The Authentic Woman

21 Self Reflections

Create a Life of Passion and Purpose Through

Emotional Wellness and Aromatherapy

Self-help Workbook

Tara Nichols, MHC, LAPC

Published by

Tara Nichols, MHC, LAPC

mentalhealth.taranichols@gmail.com

www.taranichols.com

Copyright © 2019. Tara Nichols, MHC, LAPC

First Edition

ISBN: 9781073145638

Disclaimer:

The material, products or treatments mentioned in this book are not intended to cure, diagnose, mitigate, treat or prevent any disease. Nor it is the material meant to be a substitute for professional evaluation(s) and/or treatment(s).

Self-diagnosis is never suggested as it can lead to complications if done incorrectly. You should always seek an evaluation from a qualified professional before

Cover photos courtesy of Saleen Nichols

Dedicated to the women in my life who have shared their journey with me.

My husband Derek and my sons for loving me.

And my Mom and Dad for always believing in me.

To Michele

May you live authentically

Contents

Foreword

One thing I have learned in life is how much people don't want to talk about the "skeletons in the closet". The traumas, the tragedies, the hurts and pains of our past are real. We cannot hide from them, we cannot push them into a closet and expect everything to be ok as they will sneak back up in our life in multiple ways and we must come to a point in our modern culture to start talking about these emotional pains so that we can foster a community of healing instead of being hurt people that end up hurting more people.

It is time to stop the hurting and begin the healing. Tara does an amazing job walking you through a simple path towards your own healing. This isn't easy work, but more than worth it when you walk in freedom, empowered to be the mighty Authentic Woman that you are!

As a former Army sergeant and Iraq war combat veteran and now a life coach, I understand the pains that come with traumatic experiences. I also understand what it takes to heal whole-istically by using essential oils from Young Living, a natural whole foods-based diet, supplements and having a positive belief system about myself and the world God created us to live in. The principles that Tara shares in this workbook are absolutely key to creating a healthy, happy life for yourself, despite all that you may have been through in your past.

If you are unsure about essential oils, especially in light of working through the pains of the past, I want to dispel those negative notions that they don't work. I am living proof of how powerful these little drops of love are! I have worked through my war traumas and my childhood abuse traumas and so much more, all by the grace of God and the power of God's little drops of oils! But don't take my word, try them consistently for at least 90 days as you work on your healing journey and you will be surprised by their efficacy!

One key principle that I will share as you begin this important self-work is intention. Be intentional about what you desire for your life. Be intentional about your healing, know what you see for your life on the other side of all that you are struggling with currently. Be intentional about your freedom, fight for it! Freedom is an amazing place to live in, but it comes at a price. That price is this healing work.

This heart-work in your healing is vital to understanding and respecting freedom so that you can maintain your freedom for the years to come.

It starts with you making the choice to do this work, this self-healing. Commitment is vital, commit to your journey to freedom today. Make that commitment every day and you will gain the strength needed to overcome all obstacles and heal. So, take a deep breath in and allow yourself the time and space you need to complete your healing journey and you will heal, you will walk in total emotional freedom!

It is time to link arms as a community of free people, empowering others to do the same. The ripple effect for positive change will be earth moving! Now roll up your sleeves and get to work through this amazing book by Tara!

Blessings in Christ,

Jason Sapp, MATS, CPC

www.jasonsapp.com

Introduction

The Authentic Woman is a journey of reconnecting and rediscovering our true self, the woman who has been lost or became invisible in our own lives. The woman inside of us that used to dream, laugh, play and love but somewhere along the way has been forgotten. The woman who has pushed through every challenge life has thrown her way now stands empty of hope or buried under pressure. If you find yourself a little lost, a little numb, or a little wanting for the passion you once felt for your life, or perhaps you never knew you could have a sense of passion or fulfillment and really long to understand who you are then keep reading. These 21 lessons are a collection of my experiences in learning how to find and love myself, a journey sown in pain but cultivated in hope. This is how I challenged myself to nourish love and belonging in my own life, so I could experience true connection within relationships with myself and others. This is my story.

For the woman reading this that has been broken by trauma. Beautiful woman, you have fought your whole life to be at this moment in time. Let me take a moment to tell you how courageous you are to pick up this book. To dare to be different. To say that you are done bleeding from wounds those that inflicted have long forgotten. To be willing to make small steps of change. The war might still be raging but I invite you to stop, to leave the battlefield fighting for ground you will never gain for a war that isn't yours. You are no longer caught in the barrage. I invite you to stop fighting and start living. I see you, I know you, I was you.

For the woman reading this that has done all that she can to love and support every relationship she has and now her cup is empty. Powerful woman, it is time for you to have what you need. You have given and served. Now is the time for you to overflow from a full vessel, pour into yourself. You no longer have to live in co-dependency, scarcity or fear. You are a seed completely equipped to grow into a powerful life bringing tree if only you plant yourself in an environment that allows you to have what you need. As a tree planted by rivers of water (Psalms 1, KJV), you will bear fruit from your internal gifts and not from your deeds. You are everything you need to be, together we will uncover your hearts passion and set you free. I see you, I know you, I was you.

For the woman reading this that feels stuck and simply doesn't know what is holding her back. You would like to be a better mom, wife, daughter, friend, coworker or leader but you find yourself lost and self-doubt fills your mind. You open your mouth to speak up for yourself and the words never form, you stay silent. You know what you want to do but you simply feel drained all the time and instead of making changes you use excuses to stay comfortable. You want to un-stuck yourself, but every small effort gets hi-jacked and you ask yourself "how is it all worth the effort?" I see you, I know you, I was you.

For the woman who is struggling with depression, anxiety, PTSD or other mental health diagnosis or issues. You feel lost, broken, different, or alone. You are not alone, you are not broken, and you are not a failure. The lessons in this workbook will help you find practical ways to reframe your perspective and find meaning in your patterns. You will be able to recognize and change the behaviors compounding your disorder and support a wellness lifestyle and can allow your brain to heal. Remember we are not seeking a cure, quick fix, or magic potion but a lifestyle of wellness that supports you becoming your best self. I see you, I know you, I was you.

We all share suffering in this life. Hurt people hurt people and the terrible cycle carries on through lives, families, communities, and generations. If you are reading this book, then there is something in your life that you are looking for healing or freedom from. Most of us are looking for a measure of peace. Life is filed with trauma, huge experiences leaving gaping wounds bleeding in pain and small daily disappointments that weaken the soul and numb our senses. Every woman I know has experienced some kind of pain in their life by the hand of someone they love or at their own hand. Some of us don't like to recognize our suffering because we feel that it will make us weak or vulnerable. Some of us are simply unaware that the reason we feel stuck or lost is seeded in pain. Some of us are very aware of our pain but refuse to even speak of it since we have spent so much of our lives avoiding it.

I don't want you to get hung up on a comparison game of your trauma to anyone else's story. Simply allow your mind to touch the pain that you have buried, covered with a pretty smile and soldiered through. Perhaps you are the victim of abuse, sexual assault, emotional neglect, or domestic violence. Maybe you feel shattered to the core from a haunted past. Was it a toxic relationship or a parent that hurt you? Do you just find yourself stuck, trapped in moments of fear and self-doubt? What things do you replay in your mind over and over?

Using statements like "If only I had", "I should have", or "I wish I had". Do you feel raw, exposed, tapped in every direction with nothing to give to your family, to yourself? We would be better and do better if we just knew where to start. My beautiful friend, I see you, wanting to let go and move into a better form of existence for yourself, your family, and your life. The only way you will break free from it is to HEAL from it! Keep reading.

There are three types of trauma treatment. Symptom response control is when you lessen or mute your body's natural responses to the trauma stimulus. Many treatment providers will use pharmaceutical medications to suppress pain and often the numbing dwarfs the healing process. I tend to only recommend pharmacology as an absolute last resort for trauma treatment. Many people turn to self-medicating practices as negative coping strategies. Somewhere we learned to use a bottle, plastic money, a drug, the entire cake, or a bad boy to distract us from how we feel and take our minds away from our pain, mine has always been the push and pull of a toxic relationship. In this book we will talk about natural ways to help support your body's responses to Post-Traumatic Stress and trauma.

Top down trauma treatment helps the client to control the trigger of trauma and learn coping strategies to manage symptoms moving away from helpless fear and being captive to trauma. To intellectually identify what is a normal emotion and what responses are fueled by trauma is critical to learning to live free. Cognitive Behavioral Therapists can help deconstruct negative thought patterns that keep feeding the pain and help build small meaningful behaviors to move towards hope. This type of treatment is beneficial in beginning the healing process and we will outline some solid strategies. But the healing process isn't complete without the third type of treatment.

Bottom up treatment is the experiential healing processes beginning within the person. This type of healing generates from deep within the soul and challenges their identity in trauma. The shifting of the mind to change our relationship to trauma gives us a window to redefine ourselves. Letting go is not enough. Rewriting the narrative and building meaningful identity in existence is the basis of healing. You can see how the first two treatments are helpful when used as building blocks for this final step. The exercises in this book will help unpack the trauma and pain you have survived. We cannot forget or undo the hurt you have felt. We cannot erase the scars on your heart, body, or lives. But together with hard work, we can begin writing a new chapter in your story. This form of treatment brings lasting forgiveness and peace. Cultivating this takes time and something I am learning to do for myself.

On Tuesday's I used to teach a women's trauma group for mental health and recovery. The women in my group all struggled with addiction to a chemical substance or an abusive relationship. This led to the entanglement of dysfunction, child protective services, and often the law. The women that find themselves in my room and keep showing up for themselves in class experience transformation. I have witnessed remarkable changes in lives completely shattered. I have held them as they confessed great shame for their choices. Stood by them in their grief and pain. Some of the greatest evil that they have borne in abuse. The stories of their lives leave more than finger prints on my heart. I can't even imagine how someone can bare such pain and dare to live differently. They have touched my life just by knowing them. Above all I admire their resilience.

I have noticed that they usually share a few things in common. They come in as the conditioned animal caged without chains, paralyzed by fear. At first they often start out not wanting to be there. It is not surprising that women broken in life have major trust issues and trusting a room full of female strangers seems intolerable. Like clock-work, within weeks they come to express gratitude for the opportunity to change their lives. The power of courageous women fighting to heal their families is a force that cannot be detoured by petty drama. Leading ladies that find the star roles in their lives, many were just reading the wrong script. Most of the women in my group will say that they were never asked "who they wanted to be?" or imagined a life different than the one they mindlessly ended up living. Surprisingly, they learn to trust themselves by trusting others and establish deep meaningful relationships within the group. Their shared struggle brings them closer to each other. The bonds of suffering begin to reach beyond the room and begins to repair other relationships broken in depression and isolation. It is in the emptying of their pain, the laying down of every shameful memory they can begin to experience peace. These women have taught me so much of the spirit of the warrior.

Worksheets and Narratives

This book is a collection of stories and lessons from my own healing journey that I have taught on Tuesday's to my women's group. I also use these regularly in private practice and continue them in my own life. These lessons carry the truth from the lives of these women and written with truth from my life. This book is divided into three phases. The first focuses on your past. The pain, the hurt you have experienced and still hold onto. By the end of these first steps in your healing journal you will have a trauma narrative to begin to move through the memories. The next phase focuses on rewriting your identity in your story. Creating a new script as you step into the lead role of your own star show. The final stage of this series brings each of these lessons into a commitment. By the end of the book you will have a complete narrative of the woman you are and how you came to become this amazing incredible person.

Learn to commit to the healing journey because this is only the beginning of living your most authentic life. Each exercise I have selected has been adapted to include a worksheet to help you track your journey. Take time with each step to fill out the worksheets and allow the information to seep into your soul. I would recommend only working on one lesson at a time and give yourself several days to process the information. The lessons are linear, but healing does not occur in nice neat check lists. So be open to revisiting chapters or taking addition time to rework worksheets as things come up for you. I often will take these lessons and apply them to daily frustrations or multiple situations. I started with the big stuff that kept me stuck but then I realized that the daily sacrifices of happiness or broken promises to myself were just as painful and needed the same level of care as the most painful memories. Please be gentle with yourself in this process and do not rush.

Aromatherapy

Essential oils have been an effective grounding and sensory support for reducing PTSD symptoms in therapy. At the end of every lesson we will learn how to use essential oils combined with grounding techniques that will allow you to reengage your physical body as you work through cognitive reframing. Each exercise will include a specific essential oil recommendation for its emotional release properties to support the three types of trauma treatment as you build a bottom up healing experience. I use oils in my home, with my family, and my clients. It started as my self-care and became a lifestyle of caring and kindness. As I write this I am covered in Northern Lights Black Spruce which is my most favorite of all my oils. I wanted to take a little time to introduce essential oils for anyone new to aroma therapy and talk about some important facts if you don't know much about the science.

As a brief disclaimer I am a therapist and not a medical doctor. Everything I talk about in this book is from my own uses and uses with clients, but I like to let people know up front that essential oils are very powerful when used properly to heal and support wellness in the body and mind but can also have adverse effects if you are not aware of your body and using specific oils can affect you. There are a few things you need to know about safety and usage, about farming practices and manufacturing processes that affect the potency and therapeutic properties of the oils. Oils have been used to elevate mood, regulate symptoms of hyper arousal, anxiety, stress, and support body-based regulation. Essential oils can activate the Parasympathetic Nervous System in the brain (that's the part of the brain that helps you relax) and have been used in bed time routines, homework or study practices, and remaining calm in high pressure situations. Essential oils can also activate the body's natural processes such as hormone regulation, cleansing toxins from the body, building the immune system, nutrition absorption, and even increase memory and brain function.

What Are Oils?

What are essential oils? Essential oils are the juices or life blood of every part of a plant. I spend a significant part of my spring and summer in my garden and the more I learn about plants the more I am amazed at how nature has a way of supporting life. I believe that we were created to live in a garden and essential oils are a testimony to the intelligent design of everything we need to build a healthy body, mind, and spirit. When you touch a plant or fruit on your fingers you can feel and sometimes smell the residue of that plant. Those are the oils. When steam distilled or cool pressed from the plant the oils contain all the therapeutic, emotional, and mental wellness properties that it was designed to carry. I am not a scientist but the art of extracting essential oils and using plants for healing has dated back to the beginning of civilization. Essential oils are mentioned in the Bible and other ancient text and when they would anoint someone with oil it was an act of cleansing and healing the body. They didn't do it because it smells good. Essential oils have been revived in our society and now are all the rage.

How Are Oils Different?

In gardening I have learned that most plants, just like people, adapt to the environment around them. If you have a plant raised in an organic farm then its leaves, roots, and fruit will contain less toxins and pesticides. If you have a plant grown in ground that in the past had been sprayed with chemicals to mass produce food or kill off unwanted growth, then that plant would also contain the residual toxins from that process. I think this is fascinating and speaks to the importance of good farming and awareness. It is important to know who your oil farmer is and how they are growing the plants that you will use on your body. If the oils are filled with toxins will you really want to breathe them in deeply and try to use them to carry out emotional toxins? I wouldn't.

Most essential oil companies buy their plants from third party growers which means that they really don't know how they were cultivated and if those plants contain toxins and free radicals then that will affect the quality of the oil. The second part of the process that is pretty important is the distillation. If a company is properly distilling the oils, then each essential oil will contain so many amazing benefits. If the company is cutting corners or adulterating the oil, then it decreases the effectiveness and health benefits of that oil. Unfortunately, this process is not regulated. Many companies only put 5% of pure essential oil in their product and the rest is diluted or synthetically produced to create volume. I didn't believe this at first. I put this theory to the test and bought a few bottles of oil from different providers and I was shocked at how different the same oil smelled based on how it was processed. The planting makes a difference, distillation makes a difference, and bottling makes a difference. I would strongly encourage you to research your oil providers and consider their farming practices and sourcing. Many of the easy access or seemingly affordable providers are cutting corners limiting or contaminating the healing capacity of the oil. The body's natural wellness responses to these oils are powerful when used in their unadulterated form.

I did a lot more research and there are tons of references and information out there that can give you specifics on different company practices. The connection I made from this information is that our brain, liver, and gut work to remove toxins from our bodies, both our emotional toxins and physical toxins. This work to reduce toxins and allow our brains and bodies to operate the way they were designed exhausts body function. In therapy your brain, liver, and gut control so much of your mental wellness and play a huge role in mood regulation and cognitive function. If you are using something to support your wellness, then you don't want it to also complicate the problem. We aren't trying to make your brain work harder, we are trying to give it what it needs to work well. The other part that I needed to consider was that if I was going to work to remove mental and behavioral toxins from my life then I needed to also start working on the other toxins that I was using in my lifestyle, like the plugins and products that made things smell good on the outside but were destroying my hormonal responses. I started a few years ago with a gradual change to reduce toxin exposure, period. I stopped buying things from the store that would hurt or harm my body and I stopped allowing people, places, and things in my life that would hurt or harm my spiritual and emotional wellness. I didn't do it all at once and I didn't do it quickly. This took time but one by one I reduced the sugar filled, pesticide grown, over processed foods from our cabinets and the heavy metal, toxin laden cleaning and hygiene products that I used every day. Wellness has become a lifestyle and it has allowed me to cultivate more natural processes for myself, my body, and my family.

How Do Oils Work in Therapy?

When you put a drop of essential oils on your palm and breathe in that oil its properties interact with your olfactory receptors in your sinus cavities and this sends an electrical pulse to your amygdala, the center and control tower of your brain. The brain then gets to decide what to do and how to respond to this smell. A lot like when you smell a flower that reminds you of a happy memory, essential oils can recall emotional and hormonal responses in the mind. During a therapy session we talk about some pretty heavy things, in fact most of my clients carry around heavy memories and pain every day. I did for years. When you are working through a heavy emotion and you breathe in an essential oil it allows the brain to bring more positive emotional and hormonal responses so that you are better able to regulate your physical responses to those thoughts and memories. You are able to stay fully present in your safe space while dealing with the painful memory of your past. Sometimes I don't always know why I feel certain emotions, or why my anxiety is heightened, or why thoughts of depression have taken up space in my mind but when I reach for an oil that helps me remember my internal strength and feelings of resiliency or joy I am better able to stay connected in my life.

Important Facts

Now essential oils are different than carrier oils. Carrier oils like olive oil, coconut oil, sunflower oil are fatty in nature. That is why they stain your clothes when they get on you. The heavy molecules don't evaporate and are not absorbed as quickly.

Essential oils have very small molecules that allows them to travel through the body quickly and evaporate quickly. There are three ways to use essential oils; topically, on the body; in a diffuser, which allows the oil to travel in the air; and ingested, in your food, water or in capsules. When diffused the body can absorb the oil faster as it moves through the receptors in the sinus cavity and able to transport the oil to the brain. I tend to diffuse all my oils and apply most of them topically as well. I use the diffusers to help establish a therapeutic environment in my office and my home as everyone that is breathing in the air can benefit from the oil.

1. I want to take a moment for a few cautions and safety tips that have helped me in knowing which oils to use and why. A few things you want to not do with oils. You don't want to get them in your eye, but if you do (which I have done); just apply a small amount of carrier oil to wash it out, water will make it spread so don't use water.

2. You don't want to use a "hot" oil or herbaceous oil on your skin unless you know if it will cause irritation; i.e. Peppermint, Cinnamon, Pepper, and Oregano.

3. You don't want to use photosensitive oils in direct sunlight. Citrus oils like lemon, grapefruit, and orange should be used cautiously because they will magnify the sun on your skin and cause redness or even burning. Simply apply them where the sun won't shine which is a good guide for citrus oils.

4. You want to be aware of any medical conditions you have and if certain plants or oils can affect that condition; i.e. hyssop can raise blood pressure, grapefruit can affect thyroid medications. I encourage you to research the specific oils you are using. I use PubMed and other scholarly search engines to help me understand the properties of these oils. I also follow the reference guide published by life science publishing. I have included this in my reference list at the end of this book.

5. Lastly, you want to be careful when using oils on certain populations. Children have more sensitive skin, so I usually recommend that you dilute it with a carrier oil since that will help slow the absorption rate. Use the oils on their feet as it will not get agitated by hot oils. Pets also have specific sensitivities to toxins and this is another reason to use pure therapeutic essential oils. If you

have a pet or a therapy pet in your office, then you want to know that the oils you are using will be safe around them.

I like to always be mindful of the incredible power of plants and respect that this process is more than just smelling something pretty but restoring a body and mind for wellness.

What Oils I Use

When selecting an essential oil you need to find a company that you trust. Each plant created on this earth has incredible properties and when grown organically, naturally sourced, and left unadulterated they can be incredibly powerful for the brain and body. The smell alone creates a chemical response in the brain accessing the limbic system and supporting the delicate balance between the sympathetic nervous system and parasympathetic nervous system. For these reasons I only use the highest quality of essential oils.

I started learning about essential oils 4 years ago and with all of the research I have found Young Living has the highest standards of quality and excellence. I have been using their products in my home, with my family, and with my clients for 4 years now and absolutely love the growth and changes I have seen and experienced. I have been to one of their farms and was blown away by their Seed to Seal™ commitment and the distillery and testing practices. I started using Young Living home cleaning, supplements, skin care, and hygiene products. I have seen a transformation in my family's health and wellness. I love sharing and educating women on this lifestyle and most of my friends have joined me in my journey.

If you have Young Living Essential Oils then you know exactly what I am talking about. It has been amazing, I could fill another book with the incredible information about essential oils, but I won't overwhelm you. Just know that if you want to join me and learn more about Young Living Essential Oils go to www.youngliving.com and order a starter kit. Use my member number 2740692 as your "sponsor" and "enroller". It will send me an email that you joined, and I will reach out and welcome you to our Holistic Hope team. I can't wait to walk with you on this journey.

Now that you know just enough about oils to be effective, let's dig into the workbook and start this process together. Today is the first day of moving towards living your authentic life.

For resources, references, and additional reading see the list included in the section "Where to go from here".

Section 1: Overcome

Reflection 1: Only a Symptom

In our journey toward authenticity we should always begin at the beginning, or at least where we believe the beginning to be. If you are reading this then I would venture to say that there is some part of your life that you want to change or grow. Perhaps you feel that you have lost some part of your internal passion or are needing emotional balance. We all have something we want and need healing from. Life is filled with both beautiful and painful experiences that shape us. Sometimes those experiences can dull or wound us beyond self-recognition and we are left disconnected from the person we believe and remember ourselves to be. I call this "being jaded" and all my life that seemed to be the worst possible fate, to be left jaded, misshapen by my journey and lose my inner self.

So, if you are reading this book then there is a part of your heart that is still searching to be seen, to feel understood, and to heal from your experiences. Perhaps it is an important relationship that is suffering. You may be dealing with anxiety or depression. You may even have physical responses to your trauma that is holding your life back. In my Tuesday women's group many were using substances to self-medicate and found themselves in cycles of toxic relationships. For me, I was caught in a constant replay of emotional pain. I wasn't sure if I had created the pain or attracted the dysfunction. I felt lost and jealous of everyone else's seemingly perfect life. I sized myself up on the losing end of every relationship, job, friendship, or even social encounter. I had a chip on each of my shoulders the size of Texas. I just wanted to be loved but I didn't even know how to love myself. What I didn't know is that all these things were only symptoms of a deeper problem.

You see everything you are suffering with has an original pain center. In therapy we use an intervention outlining an activating event triggering a belief about ourselves that leads us to a response. Our brain wants to prove our cognitive structures and validate how we are responding. We look for evidence that our thought patterns are correct and begin recalling memories to support our core beliefs. These beliefs and memories soon become tied as a repeating pattern leading to a growing list of experiences backing up our self-authoring truth. This is a great process if we are growing up in a positive life, filled with support. Then our core beliefs are founded on compassion and positive regard for self and others. But, if you grew up with trauma, pain, or abuse then your core beliefs have been damaged. Most likely your self-image has changed and when your brain recalls memories they are filled with fear and pain. These patterns repeat throughout your life, your relationships, and even your mind. If you took the time to even listen to your mind's replay you might pick out a few of these repeating negative beliefs about yourself. Like a broken record they play over and over and repeat themselves in your relationships, your interactions on the job, your social interactions, your health choices, and every part of your life. You would like to change. You would like to simply make different choices, but you aren't exactly sure where or when this all started. Let's untangle this mess. Let's slow down the record and deconstruct the audio.

Take a few minutes to write out the symptoms you are struggling with.

_____

_____

_____

(Examples might be: insomnia, poor diet, anxiety, loss, anger, depression, etc.)

Now ask yourself for each corresponding symptom what fear is driving the response. This might be hard at first. For me one of my symptoms was anxiety in my relationships. The fear that propelled that behavior was the fear of being alone. I also dealt with negative self-talk. I treated myself as if I was the absolute worst person I knew. I was never kind to myself in my thoughts. I feared rejection and judgement. I motivated myself through strong self-criticism. I knew that if I had told myself how unworthy I was then perhaps it wouldn't hurt so badly if I wasn't accepted by that social group or didn't make the grade. I had a very hard time processing disappointment of others. Fear governed my life and I wasn't even aware of its presence in my thoughts. Take some time now to match up your fears with each of your symptoms.

_____

_____

_____

(Examples might be: rejection, loneliness, success, loss, failure, not being enough, etc.)

Moving one layer deeper let's begin uncovering our needs. The unmet needs in our life play a great role in fueling our behaviors. As creatures of instinct we are driven to meet our own needs. Positive and maladaptive behaviors are driven by meeting needs. Maslow laid out a hierarchy of needs stating that all humans have five basic needs. The need for survival, safety, love or belonging, purpose, and self-actualization. With each of our fears our inner self is reaching out to have our unmet needs satisfied. We just want to feel whole again, to not be walking around starving for these basic things necessary for fulfillment. We want to be loved, to belong, to have purpose or meaning, to feel safe in our own skin. When I realized how much my heart just yearned to belong I felt that I had uncovered a hidden secret. A dark truth of my vulnerability. It was more than finding a boyfriend or wanting to have kids. I had never in my life experienced true understanding. And I hadn't given myself that understanding either. I needed to feel acceptance for exactly who I was, imperfect as I am. All my pain symptoms and all my fear didn't matter because under each of those bad behaviors and desperation, I had an unmet need at the core of my existence. So, ask yourself what are you needing? What is missing in your life that drives your fears?

List that need or needs here:

_____

_____

_____

_____

As you are traveling deeper into your self-understanding and memories ask yourself this one question, when did all this start? What is your original pain center? What is your earliest memory of that need you listed above being something you desired? How old were you? Most likely you were in early childhood and more often than not this wound begins at home. Our family are often part of our pain cycles. Think back to that core belief you formed about yourself. For me, my mom abandoned me as a toddler. There were courts and paperwork and all kinds of things a child doesn't understand but it was years before I would see her. Loss and abandonment were at the core of my symptomology. I had grown up expecting rejection and pain, so I set up relationships to fail to validate the pain I felt. I had created the cage I lived in with the doors unlocked but I had walled myself in.

Write down your first memories of pain.

_____

_____

_____

_____

Now let's fill in the chart with each of your answers to build their connection in a visual form.

```
        Symptom  _____  _____

          Fear   _____  _____

          Need   _____  _____

          Pain
```

You have now completed your first day. Your first step in understanding your trauma process. From this chart you can trace so many symptomatic behaviors. This is a system you can also use to help understand other people's behaviors. Begin looking at the deeper fears motivating your relationships and the needs people are looking to fill in their lives. Ask yourself, what fears are you acting on every day? How can you recognize and meet your own needs?

Additional Thoughts:

_____

_____

_____

_____

_____

_____

_____

_____

Essential Oil and Grounding Intervention:

Black Spruce or Bergamot

As mentioned in the introduction we will be using natural interventions to provide a positive coping mechanism to soften the biological responses to your trauma memories. As you move through your pain memories and sift through your fears, your trauma is being triggered and exposed. Keep in mind to be gentle with yourself. Using an essential oil intervention can access the amygdala of the brain and support sensory grounding. Creating a safe place in your mind to begin processing your pain can allow for more intentionality in your responses.

Take your essential oil, for this exercise I recommend black spruce or bergamot. Drop one drop into your palm. Rotate the oil with your other hand and cup your palms. Using your inward and outward breaths, breathe deeply cupping the oil over your nose and mouth. Breath in nasally, hold your breath for three seconds. Exhale from your gut pushing your breath out through your mouth and release the pain out of your body. Imagine the air going down to the part of your body where you feel the deepest pain. If it is in your chest, belly, or pelvis. The molecules of the cleansing breath and oil reach deep inside your cells and pull out the pain. We open ourselves up and force the pain forward. With each breath we breathe in peace and then release the suffering.

Write down the oil that you used and what it reminds you of:

_____

_____

_____

_____

_____

Additional thoughts:

_____

_____

_____

_____

_____

_____

_____

_____

_____

_____

_____

_____

_____

_____

Overcome

Reflection 2: The Brain as an Airport

The brain develops from bottom up. I like to say that the brain is like an airport. It starts with a central hub, the brain stem. At the top of the brain stem is the amygdala, the brain's control tower. That is the part of your brain responsible for your hormone control, memory storage, and emotional regulation. Information coming into the brain is like airplanes. As information comes in, the brain assesses the current terminals and decides if the plane can be routed to an existing memory. If not, the brain builds a new terminal. During early childhood new experiences expand the brain at rapid rates. Therefore, it is critical to expose your children to discovery learning and developmental play. Off each terminal the brain categorizes information into gates and builds pathways between the gates and reroutes information.

A good example of this is a ball. When you were a child you were most likely introduced to a ball of some kind. This small round object that might bounce, over time becomes an entire category of sports, experiences, expectations, memories of catching, throwing, missing, being hurt, wins or loses, an entire life can be built on the simple terminal tied to that first memory of a ball. But as a person grows if the terminals are left empty or unused the brain shuts down those terminals. They are not destroyed but left vacant.

If you never play with a ball after your first experience and instead take other paths, then you most likely have lost immediate recollection to those memories. If your father was an alcoholic who ignored you during football seasons and screamed at the television, then perhaps your terminal title "ball and all things related" is one that is filled with gates leading to sadness. Your relationships and experiences pass through the corridors of your airport looking for where they fit.

There are a few things that can hi-jack your airport, take command of your control tower, over surge your amygdala. Drugs, toxic emotional relationships, abuse and trauma all have the power to shut down large sections of the brain. The amygdala can go into overdrive and strong emotional responses or a flood of chemicals in the brain can create damage to your terminals. The brain might not even recognize the changes but as efficiently as possible start redirecting information through the new terminal of trauma, abuse, or chemical addiction.

Before long the trauma terminal becomes a security checkpoint in which all passengers, active flight paths, and information is passed through its gates. The greater the violation or complexity of the trauma the greater the security procedures. The problem is that you can't simply shut down that part of your brain without rerouting how the brain processes the information and experiences flying into our lives. It takes time to begin rebuilding, reconnecting, and reviving the parts of our brain that we have lost or forgotten. Or have been numbed by the trauma, pain, or substance abuse.

If you flew into Atlanta in the last few months you would have noticed the major construction on the North Terminal. The idea that a brain can be repaired is very real. Neuroplasticity means that your brain can regrow and repair itself. It allows for healing of the neurological pathways. Just like the brain, the airport doesn't shut down during construction but having a plan and a skilled construction manager is critical. Understanding how our brain works should both create gratitude for this incredible organ but also create a sense of responsibility. We have a right to how we feel but the reality is that we also have a responsibility to our brain. We have a responsibility to help support healthy emotional responses. This might be as long and as painful as the reconstruction of the North Terminal. But it is our responsibility and absolutely a critical part of healing.

Take some time to think back to the thoughts that race and the emotions that take control of your control tower. Write down some of the feelings corresponding with each of the topics in the chart and add a few of your own. You know your brain, just listen.

(See chart next page.)

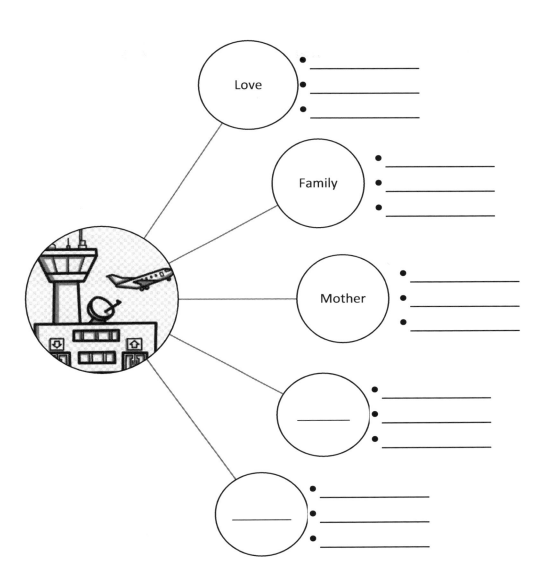

Love

Family

Mother

You may find that as you are filling out this chart you notice patterns of trauma in your information processing. If you pick up on relationships between experiences and pain, then take notice. You may want to write down some of your thoughts. Keep your mind open. Don't restrict yourself to the few lines above. Add all the space you need. Take time to be fully aware in this moment.

Ask yourself throughout the day how many interactions are seen through the terminal of trauma. How often are your security checkpoints alerted and in which relationships do you feel safe?

_____

_____

_____

_____

Additional Thoughts:

_____

_____

_____

_____

_____

_____

_____

_____

_____

_____

_____

_____

_____

Essential Oil and Grounding Intervention:

Frankincense

Frankincense is an amazing brain oil. Using oils that support cognitive functioning and help pull you through your emotional responses to a logical understanding can support this process. Remember to use the cupping strategy we introduced in the last step with each oil you use. You can also place a drop of oil on your temples and the top of your head. You have olfactory sensors that transmit the oils as an electrical pulse to the brain. Using specific oils can increase brain activity. Meditation and mindfulness can also increase the production of brainwaves in areas of the brain that have been shut down by trauma.

Keep in mind that the amount of time in meditation is an important part of engaging neuroplasticity. Start a timer when you begin, be thoughtful of increasing your meditation lengths. Begin small and with every breath draw out each movement. Expand yourself in your space, breath longer, hold your pose and slow your mind. Begin to be thoughtful each day lengthening the time you give to yourself and your brain. List the oils you used and how long you meditated.

Today I used: _____

Length of time meditating: _____

Additional thoughts:

_____

_____

_____

_____

_____

_____

_____

_____

_____

Overcome

Reflection 3: Illusions of Safety

You're making huge progress. The first and second lessons in this book are indeed heavy. If you find yourself exhausted after worksheet and exercise don't be surprised. Remember to give yourself time. You are healing, you are learning. This is no different than entering a scholastic program or mountain climbing. Many will hike the Appalachian Trail and not work as hard as you will to uncover and heal from trauma. So we take one step at a time and rest when we are exhausted. Today we will talk about expectations and how holding on to disappointments are only illusions for control and safety.

Many are making the connection between controlling behaviors and anxiety. The trouble with PTSD, stress, and trauma is that it creates opening doors for co-occurring disorders and anxiety is highly prevalent. Understanding this is great but what does it look like for our lives? Anxiety medications are so highly prescribed that most don't think twice about asking a doctor for a pill to manage daily interactions. Our lives are flooded with small stresses that build and overwhelm us and we tell ourselves that if we could only have more control over relationships, careers, or our families then we would have less worry. My son told me about an April fools' prank that included setting up hundreds of plastic cups covering the floor filled with water. As a person walks across their room they have no choice but to knock over a percentage of the cups spilling other cups, more and more water slipping and splashing across the floor. For a child this sounds hilarious but for a mom this is cruel and unusual torture.

The reality is that a life in anxiety can feel very much like that person standing in the middle of the room filled with plastic cups and a short trail of turned over cups behind us leading back to bed. The twisted part is that those tiny cups of water are usually placed there by our own doing. The cups represent our expectations of ourselves and others. We think that if we can control our environment then we will be safe from our trauma. Our fear of having unmet needs motivate the placement of a tiny thirst-quenching receptacle. Before long we have a thousand cups scattered through the room and we have lost the ability to maneuver in our own lives. Many days we wake up and simply don't feel like handling the damage control that has become our life. We allow depression to sink in and we shrink from the day. We might think that if we pick up each cup carefully and shift the water that we can make it to the other side and we are exhausted from trying to control the outcome. We could decide to start drinking each cup one at a time and we internalize the anxiety but then the water won't be there for the future, and before long we would be running for the bathroom. Regardless of how we cope with our situation we must face the fact that we are now resentful and trapped by our own making. When we look to outside sources to meet our needs we are building a cage of co-dependence. Instead of trusting our ability to find and source "water" for ourselves we become reliant on a system that keeps us in the cycle of depression and anxiety. Our need for the illusion of safety feeds our desire for control.

Below is a diagram of the things you fight to control. Think of the disappointments you hold on to everyday. Think of the relationships that fuel your feelings of resentment. Of the people or outcomes that you are trying to manipulate. List some of the daily expectations that keep you feeling trapped. What would happen if you just released the control of one of these items? Is it your kids, your spouse, or you co-workers? If you shifted your expectations and took that "cup of water" pouring it out into a nearby plant or sink? If you took the energy you used on that relationship as something to control and let go of any expectations, what do you

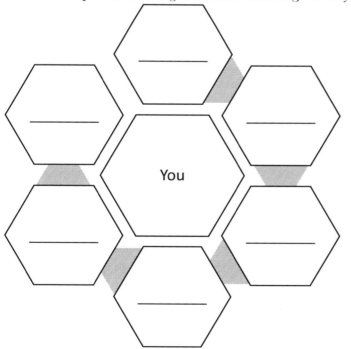

think would happen? This might sound terrifying but let's play out the possibilities. It you stopped focusing so much on things you can't control. You can't control your children's behaviors. You can model, teach, limit, and encourage. That's pretty much the extent of your influence. The only person you can control is you. Your interactions and responses to the scenario. Next, take some time to consider three scenarios that trigger your anxiety based on the relationships listed in the graph above. Write out both the positive and negative possibilities and your responses. The goal is to identify the anxiety patterns so that we understand and release them. Also, list at least one identified support person that you would be able to contact for help.

Scenario 1:

_____

_____

Positive - Expected Outcome:

_____

Response:

_____

Negative - Expected Outcome:

_____

Response:

_____

Support person:

_____

Contact:

_____

Scenario 2:

_____

_____

Positive - Expected Outcome:

_____

Response:

_____

Negative - Expected Outcome:

_____

Response:

_____

Support person:

_____

Contact:

_____

Scenario 3:

_____

_____

Positive - Expected Outcome:

_____

Response:

_____

Negative - Expected Outcome:

_____

Response:

_____

Support person:

_____

Contact:

_____

How do you see this affecting your relationship? How do you think this will impact you? Are you willing to trust that based on your responses and the support person you have identified that you would stay safe? Sometimes letting go of co-dependency and expectations takes time. Many of our expectations are tied to a false sense of entitlement rather than self-compassion. When we empty ourselves of demands we can walk in gratitude. Sometimes naming the emotional process is enough to begin to release them.

Additional thoughts:

_____

_____

_____

_____

_____

_____

_____

_____

_____

Essential Oil and Grounding Intervention:

Sandalwood

Bringing up hurtful memories can take our minds back into the past and we can feel isolated from our current lives. It is important when doing these lessons that you practice grounding yourself in today. One of the essential oils I like to use for this is sandalwood because it helps build feelings of connectivity and removes feelings of isolation. It is so easy to isolate ourselves from difficult or vulnerable feelings and anxiety plays a huge role in keeping us trapped in those thoughts. For this grounding exercise we will learn to reconnect with our surroundings. Using the sense of sight allow your mind to focus on the objects with you in the room. You are safe. You are not in your past pain. Be fully present where you are and allow your mind to remember the past as it is, a memory, not a current event.

Place a drop of oil in your palm for the cupping exercise from the first lesson and begin recognizing 5 objects you can see, name them. State out loud 4 facts about the room you are in. Name 3 things you did to be in this room. Remember to breathe through this exercise while cupping your oil. Name 2 things your body feels in this moment. Feel your heart beat slow and your tension release. Breathe and say a self-affirmation about yourself in this moment.

Remember to use this grounding mechanism throughout the next few days. As you begin working on your deep memories and begin bringing them to the surface of your mind, you may experience symptoms of post-traumatic stress. Take time every day to practice grounding your emotions in the present. Connect your mind to your physical experiences and remember you are safe, growing, and learning more and more about yourself in this process.

Additional thoughts:

_____

_____

_____

_____

_____

_____

_____

_____

_____

_____

_____

Overcome

Reflection 4: Whispering Forgiveness

We have spent the last few days digging up some very deep and dark feelings. Powerful emotions and nasty memories. I know that when I began to therapeutically process my childhood trauma and relationship failures the realization of my role in perpetuating the cycle knocked me back. The hardest part was not that the people I loved hurt me, I still loved those people. The hardest part was that I had hurt myself, and I had stopped loving myself. The suffering I felt had become my identity and I leveraged that pain in all my relationships. I justified my bad behaviors, my self-doubt, self-criticism, jealousy, and every negative thought under the white flag of childhood trauma. I surrendered my life by living mindlessly reactive instead of intentionally. I had asked God for forgiveness. I was open to the idea that my higher power could carry my pain. But the idea that the existence of that higher power in me; the divine presence of that Higher Power working inside of me to create greatness was just too much. People would tell me that classic phrase, "you have to forgive and let go", "and forgiveness is for yourself". I know we have all read a dozen meme's on what forgiveness looks like but until you have walked this journey you can't comprehend the gravity and fear that comes with letting go of our pain and emptiness from our trauma.

As mentioned in lesson 2 the brain shifts to filter all our experiences through a trauma lens. The experience of becoming a victim to trauma fuses with our personal truths and core beliefs. We can adopt a victim identity. "Bad things happen to me" and people "hurt me". The idea of forgiveness threatens the concept that we could then leverage that painful experience to justify current states of emotional existence. Practicing forgiveness is an exercise of faith that a greater purpose would then offer meaningfulness to the pain. Until we can embrace the possibility of a new identity in healing from trauma, forgiveness is cognitively out of reach. Forgiving others begins with allowing ourselves to stop leveraging the pain as part of our identity. Being willing to set aside the pain and opening our mind to moving through the pain. We must be willing to see ourselves as a survivor, overcomer, and free from the experience of the betrayal. We have heard that people's behaviors say more about them than it does us. But how does the help us set down the hurting and move towards forgiveness?

So where do we begin to forgive? For me my faith had to become bigger than my pain. The idea that everything I had suffered could be used for something meaningful. The realization that only by healing could I move into a place of purpose. I began with a whisper I was so hurt that speaking it out loud or in conversation was too difficult at first. But whispering "I forgive __ " and the person's name would catch in my throat. I began focusing on imagining forgiveness as an existence rather than a targeted action. If I didn't have to point my forgiveness at a person, then I could just try walking in forgiveness. Somedays were easier than others. Some days seemed almost impossible and self-doubt took over my thoughts. I would say "but you don't understand, if I forgive this person then people won't know how they hurt me; how much I have had to overcome. People won't understand my pain." I would meet people and the shame of my trauma would overtake my mind and I would whisper under my breath, "I live in forgiveness and I forgive myself."

Whispered prayers of the heart are soon shouted. In each moment of disbelief that we could set aside the rejection and abandonment, we whisper. The wounded story we tell ourselves slowly begins to change. Our voice becomes louder. We begin to put actions behind our words that were once whispers and slowly we truly live forgiveness. Walking in forgiveness is the act of living out a life built on an identity of hope rather than holding on to the wounds of the past. When we walk in forgiveness we are living out freedom from the hurt. Forgiveness does not release the perpetrator of guilt, but it removes the shame from the victim and breaks the cycle of abuse. I am no longer bound by my shame for decisions that kept me in a victim identity and cycle of abuse. My whispers are a battle cry of freedom.

Write down at least three relationships or decisions you are going to forgive yourself for.

1. _____

2. _____

3. _____

Write down three people that you intend to walk in forgiveness towards.

1. _____

2. _____

3. _____

Write down your whispers.

1. _____

2. _____

3. _____

Additional thoughts:

_____

_____

_____

_____

_____

_____

_____

_____

_____

Essential Oil and Grounding Intervention:

German Chamomile

Reconnecting from detachment: In this grounding exercise we will learn to breathe the essential oil German Chamomile. German Chamomile is an herb known for its relaxation qualities, but it helps reconnect from feelings of disassociation. As we focus on forgiveness the pain can overwhelm our process. The fear is that our trauma is an iceberg and our deepest pain is greater than we can manage. Our brain will do what it can to avoid and detach from our feelings, our physical sensations, and our own lives. This can build over time and compound the healing process, bring us to a place where we feel lost as if we don't know who we are.

To reconnect with your authentic self, you begin with your breathing. Most of our exercises will center on breathing. The Greek word for breath means soul or spirit. Your breath is your life. Place German Chamomile in your palm and breathe in deeply. Take your thoughts and picture them reentering and reconnecting to your body. Focus on you as you breathe. Feel the air as it enters your lungs, hold your spirit inside of you and allow that breath to enter you, pulling out the painful memory and as you exhale push that pain out.

Let's do this again, I know you are still holding your pain deep inside of you. Breathe in, feel that cleansing air, hold that life deep in your belly, pull that pain from your gut and force it out. One more time, now let's connect your arms to the process, as you put your arms in front of you, palms up reach for the life you want and pull it close to your heart as you breathe in. Pull with courage, let your arms hold that spirit close to your heart pulling your elbows back behind you and expanding your lungs. Hold that breath and allow it to travel down to your roots, "I breathe in life". Now with all your force, push your arms forward and exhale "I release my pain".

Each time you practice this exercise focus on connecting to your body and to your pain so that you can bring it out of your depths pushing it out to be cleansed by the air. Do not disconnect from the pain that is buried, release it.

We feel so that we can heal.

Overcome

Reflection 5: Shame and Guilt

We are all intimately familiar with the concept of shame and guilt. In fact, shame and guilt are huge motivators for our behaviors. When you look at these deeply painful feelings objectively, without judgement, we can learn a lot from our shame. I read once that the different between shame and guilt is that guilt motivates feelings of responsibility and restitution whereas shame is tied to our state of existence. I felt that this helped distinguish some of my feelings and my responses to situations. The more I became open to understanding the thoughts seeded in shame or the behaviors manipulated by guilt, the more I could untangle my patterns.

When I meditate on deep emotions I imagine a basement underneath a house. When I was a child we lived in Purcell, Oklahoma. There is an old house there built in 1903. One of its previous owners had set fire to the basement to collect on some insurance policy. The house never burned but that basement was the most terrifying. The walls and doors were black from the fire. It had the smell of charcoal. I imagine a basement like this. Black burn marks, cobwebs, darkness; fear, shame, and guilt all tossed in my psychological "basement" like unwanted furnishings or old belongings. Emotions can be overwhelming, and it becomes so easy to tuck them away in corners of our psyches.

I know I was too afraid of my own darkness to actually take care of what was hurting me. I had far more important things to do than to declutter an "emotions" infested basement. I spent my time making the parts of my life that were visible as attractive as possible. If no one knew I was operating through guilt for things that destroyed my sense of self, I wouldn't be known as an impostor. I used my strengths in relationships and most of my friends never knew the pain that was building on the inside. The terrible truth about moldy, unmanaged basements is that the decay spreads. Any part of your emotional health that is ignored will fester are create dysfunctional patterns.

The first part of healing is being willing to begin the decluttering process. Starting one memory at a time, one core belief, one painful experience. Sometimes we don't have to unpack everything at once but if we start with isolated moments in time and take care of each emotional response we can begin to heal. Below is a graph to help simplify the "clean-up" process. We will begin untangling complex trauma and deep emotions so prepare yourself with the grounding exercises you have learned. Oil up with your favorite essential oil and calm your heart and mind.

Now, take a few moments to focus on a memory that you hide in your "basement". One that keeps you terrified to even open the door to walk down the stairs. Imagine yourself walking to your basement and reaching in to turn on the light. What is the one memory that comes to your mind at first? Write that experience in the trauma blank below. Can you recognize any beliefs about yourself that stem from this memory? What are the corresponding thoughts coming to mind as this is being recalled? Identify the shame you felt and if you felt guilt associated with needing to "fix" or repair the situation. Fill in any actions fueled by that guilt.

Trauma

Trauma memory:
_____
_____
_____

Beliefs about myself...
_____
_____
_____

Choices I made...
_____
_____

People affected...
_____
_____
_____

Shame

Shame you felt:
_____
_____

I am bad because...
_____
_____

I don't deserve...
_____
_____

I blame myself for...
_____
_____
_____

Guilt

Guilt driven behavior:
_____
_____

This is my fault...
_____
_____

I am a failure when...
_____
_____

Things I would fix...
_____
_____

Looking at your shame as part of how you view your personal identity can help you begin separating out what thoughts about yourself are true and what are stemming from your trauma. Taking assessment of the difference between shame and guilt can help outline the behaviors in relationships that we are modeling because of old trauma patterns. How you respond to your trauma can continue to impact your relationships today because you still carry the shame and guilt of your past. Take a few moments to think on these questions. You may have a few thoughts of your own. Please take time to write them down as well.

Current thoughts about my shame and guilt:

_____

_____

_____

_____

_____

Lies I tell myself that are fueled by my shame:

_____

_____

_____

_____

Truthful beliefs that can help me let go of shame:

_____

_____

_____

_____

Shame is a profound emotional response and is embedded in a lack of empathy for ourselves. The antidote to shame is compassion. In future lessons we will focus on cultivating compassion for ourselves but for now begin recognizing how shame plays a role in your life and as you are able to label shame and guilt motivated behaviors you will be able to make a clear distinction between your authentic responses and responses manipulated out of that shame and guilt.

Many people find that they are not living an authentic life because they are compromised by these deep terrible emotions rooted in the lies of a broken self-truth. How can we respond as our true self if we are so compromised by this darkness? Take time each day to walk to your mental basement, bring forward a forgotten emotion and mentally acknowledge that feeling. Take time to recognize these feelings as part of you. Access what you no longer need in your basement because you don't feel bound by those feelings anymore, clean those out of your mental storage space.

Be kind to yourself and repackage your heavy and hard feelings in a way that they are cared for, not feared. You might not be able to rid yourself of all shame, guilt, resentment, anger in one trip to your basement. So, take one emotion to focus on. Label what you can recall. "This was done out of my guilt, I will forgive myself for allowing my emotions to control my responses. I will recognize what is driving my reactions. I will take care of my feelings today." Remember to tidy your emotional basement and then return to the rest of your life. Don't stay in the darkness, you will be able to return tomorrow and work on another feeling, but your life awaits you and you don't have to let these painful emotions control your life anymore.

What emotions are you working on today?

_____

_____

What are the dark feelings that you are afraid to focus on?

_____

_____

As you begin to clean up your emotional basement, what emotions would you like to make more room for in your life?

_____

_____

Additional Thoughts:

_____

_____

Essential Oil and Grounding Intervention:

Lemon

I know these emotions are powerful and vulnerability is terrifying. Sometimes we hold on to our feelings of shame because we feel that we would be empty without it and emptiness is more terrifying than anything else. Lemon essential oil helps to release feelings of emptiness, regret, and sadness. Lemon is a cleansing agent and helps the body purify from toxins. Lemon is one of the oils I love to diffuse or use with a carrier oil. It is photosensitive, so I am careful to not use it in the sun. Be mindful of your emotions and the fear of letting go of what you have, even if what you have is hurting you.

Breathe in lemon essential oil diffused. Open your heart to allow yourself to meditate on beginning to reframe or "clean" the memories of shame and guilt. As in the exercise of this lesson meditate on allowing yourself to re-center the memory and its emotion from a cleansing perspective.

As each memory comes to mind allow your mind to see it from a clear perspective, begin removing the shame and allow yourself to only see the facts of the memories, the story as it was. Recall details of the events and place them in equal relevance to the emotions of the time.

Allow yourself to cleanse your memory from judgement and regret and place the memory back into your mind as it should be, as recalling of a fact. Bring your current emotions to the present and don't leave them in the details of the past.

"Today I feel sad because I remember the facts of my childhood." *Breathe*

"I can be kind to myself today. I can heal because today I am an older, stronger, kinder adult." *Breathe*

"I have empathy for my younger self, the child in my memory. I remove shame from that child." Breathe

"I cleanse myself of my guilt. I will take time for my emotions every day." *Breathe*

Additional thoughts:

_____

_____

_____

_____

_____

_____

_____

_____

_____

_____

_____

_____

_____

_____

_____

_____

_____

_____

Overcome

Reflection 6: Our Self Scripts

In therapy there is a technique used to understand self-identity called transactional theory. It outlines the inner self as three main voices. The inner critic, the inner parent, and the inner child. The inner critic is our voice of judgement, the part of us that is looking for errors, flaws, or weak points. This voice can often be a helpful force in helping us improve on our behaviors, to challenge us to be better. This inner voice can also be harmful when it is based in shame and wounded personal identity. The inner child is our young self. The earliest memories you have of your personality and how you navigated the world. Like the critic, the strengths of your inner child are often profound in building our ambitions, dreams, and closest relationships. The inner child often is the simplest of our internal processes and if we listen it can give us clues to our needs and desires.

If you have experienced a lot of trauma during your childhood you may not have a strong inner child voice. This voice can be shut out or you may experience that part of you are difficult to listen to. I felt my inner child's voice was always based in self-pity. It was hard to be an independent adult and listen to an inner child that felt abandoned all the time. This left me treating myself even more unkindly in my own head.

Last, we have the nurturing parent as caretaker of our souls. This is our problem solver, comforter, and encourager. The parents help us filter what the inner critic is telling us and put it into action to support the inner child. Sometimes though, the nurturing parent can become passive or enabling. If we are not recognizing our own roles and responsibilities then these thought patterns can feed co-dependency. This can be very destructive to our relationships. The balance between these three voices is critical for a balanced mindset. The words and thoughts carried out in our own minds will drive our behaviors towards ourselves and others. Often, we cannot begin building the life we want because we cannot balance the relationship we have with our inner self and that imbalance pours out into our relationships in life. Our toxic mindset towards ourselves drives us to seek and cultivate toxic patterns in work, home, and friend relationships. It allows our brains to feel comfortable in the chaos that is our mind.

In my Tuesday class we practice listening to our self-script. Inside our heads we often have a script that we recite to ourselves. Like a play each internal voice is handed a script to read during times of emotional response. Sometimes this script is handed down from our family, our parents or relatives, and sometimes this script is something we have gathered through our experiences. If you listen closely to the messages that you often find yourself saying in your own mind you can usually pick out which inner self is doing the most "talking". Take a few moments to stop and think back to your last difficult situation. Perhaps you were stressed at work, maybe there was an issue with your family, or maybe you were at lunch with a friend and were having a difficult conversation. What was playing through your mind? What things do you tell yourself? Write down how you would answer these questions.

What do you tell yourself about your body?

_____

_____

What do you tell yourself about your education/intelligence?

_____

_____

What do you tell yourself about how you treat your children?

_____

_____

How do you talk to yourself about mistakes?

_____

_____

What do you say to yourself about your marriage/relationship?

_____

_____

How do you talk to yourself about sex or intimacy?

_____

_____

Our inner voices play major roles in how we navigate our experiences. If we can listen and are mindful of the inner scripts we repeat, then we have the power of self-awareness to what our internal processes are needing. The relationship between our inner self and how we treat our inner voices is often built and amplified through a cycle of repeat experiences. If our inner critic is cruel and amplifies our shame, the inner nurturer tries to over compensate with self-indulgent thoughts, and our inner child crumbles in self-doubt and sadness.

We experience a stressful situation at work, our inner critic recalls all the failures of our day, week, and even our career. The nurturer attempts to distract or sooth our stress response and shame with rationalizations. And our inner child retreats to pain and isolation. Understanding the internal process helps to identify how we are perpetuating the abuse cycle internally. We take the experiences from our relationships and begin treating ourselves with the same hostility.

Some women have a very difficult time hearing their inner child. Because of unspoken abuse they have felt their inner child silenced. Learning to listen and allow each part of our person to be heard. I encourage women to sit with themselves. If they are struggling with hearing their inner child then they need to go to places that would specifically bring out childhood emotions such as joy, happiness, and laughter. They should create opportunities to feel at peace, read children's story books, and eat desert before dinner.

Allow the inner child to exist without judgement and then stay open to the feelings that begin to flow. Be mindful of the patterns in the cycles of your experiences. Taking a few of the questions I asked above begin to fill out your internal scripts. Remember just to listen, don't judge the voice, listen and learn openly.

What do you tell yourself about your body?

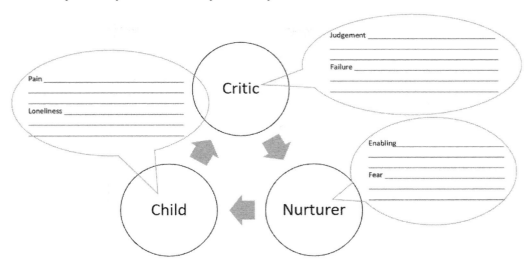

What do you tell yourself about your mistakes?

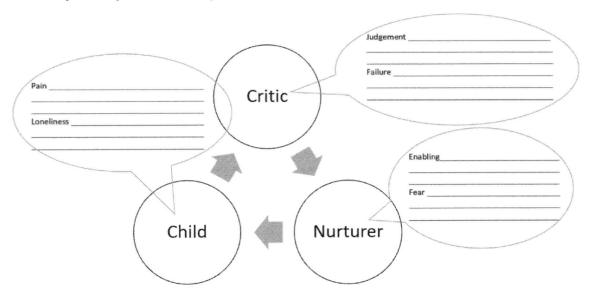

What do you tell yourself about how you parent?

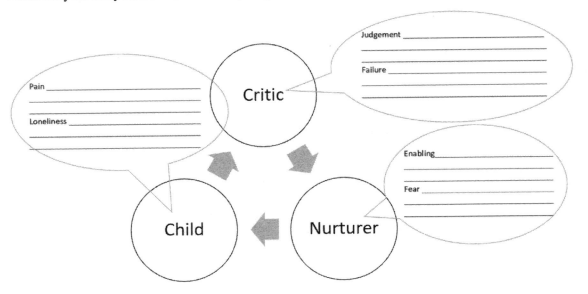

Now begin to look for patterns in the way you talk to yourself. Is the script in your head critical, nurturing, or child like? Do you see a balance between the inner voices? Do you feel that any of the voices are silent or can't be heard? Do you see anything you would like to change about the way to talk to yourself?

Which voice is the loudest?

_____

Does your inner voice sound like someone from your life?

_____

How does this inner voice affect you?

_____

_____

_____

_____

_____

_____

How does this inner voice affect how you feel in your relationships?

_____

_____

_____

_____

_____

What would you like to change about your inner self script?

_____

_____

_____

Additional thoughts:

_____

_____

_____

_____

_____

_____

_____

_____

_____

_____

_____

_____

_____

Essential Oil and Grounding Intervention:

Orange

Like other essential oils, Orange contains wonderful properties for cleansing the body and releasing emotions of anger, hostility, and ridicule. This lesson holds one of the most profound insights into what is holding you back from your authentic life, the words you use towards yourselves. Often these words are so unspeakable that we wouldn't talk to anyone we know in this manner.

We often verbally attack and emotionally abuse our self, breaking our own promises and tearing down our own dreams. So much energy we waste rebuilding our internal spirit after we just demolished our own motivation with these cruel self-directed conversations. For this intervention we will practice affirmations while deep breathing our essential oil.

Notice I didn't use the words "positive affirmation" because we don't always feel positive about ourselves and the last thing we want to do is lie. The negative and cruel words we use to hurt ourselves are lies, why would we cover them over with prettier lies? So, for every negative thought I want you to stop, examine the thought, remove the lie with an "I am not" statement, and speak an affirmation of a personal truth.

This might be hard at first. You may need to write a few down to help you remember when you are struggling. Remember to breathe a drop of orange oil or use this oil in a diffuser to lift your spirit as you are working through the cognitive processes and reprogramming your internal speech.

What I tell myself

_____

_____

I am not

_____

_____

What is true about me

_____

What I tell myself

_____

I am not

_____

What is true about me

_____

What I tell myself

_____

I am not

_____

What is true about me

_____

Additional thoughts:

_____

_____

_____

Overcome

Reflection 7: The Cycle within Us

This is the last lesson in section 1. My prayer is that you have learned so much about yourself, your thought patterns and the beliefs you hold about yourself. We might not love or even like the way we think and feel about ourselves at this part of the trauma healing process but recognizing these thoughts can give us knowledge and power to change. Take a moment to be exactly where you are emotionally. You are right where you need to be in your journey. Give yourself a big hug and keep moving forward.

In this lesson we are going to examine how the abuse cycle is created and how by holding on to abuse we can reinforce a victim ideology and narrative for our lives that we repeat without awareness. I know we have all experienced deeply painful moments. We are working through our trauma because that pain has taken over some part of our life and holds us back from living in freedom. Life is filled with moments of suffering but when that suffering becomes our identity we lose power over who we are and find ourselves in toxic relationships and situations. We become a suffering person rather than a person moving through suffering. As you are removing toxic thoughts and emotions we can start looking at toxic relationships in our life.

Most relationships do not begin in toxic patterns. Most begin with small infractions or co-dependent patterns that we overlook. Think of a time in the beginning stages of a relationship when you first noticed that you were treated badly. Perhaps it was something small, a crossing of a boundary or a verbal argument. Because you cared about the person and perhaps you felt shame based on the event, you just took the pain. Maybe the event sounded so much like the inner self script that you believed you deserved the mistreatment. The beliefs you hold about yourself influence the level of pain you are willing to receive from others. So, you take it the first time. You leverage your internal strength and twist that up with your shame and guilt. You think, "I can take this, it wasn't that bad". That person must "need to be loved" more. Sometimes our understanding of what love really means is so twisted that we can't even recognize the difference between love and toxic behavior. Now that you have the memory in your mind let's write this down.

Bad Behavior Memory:

_____

_____

_____

Shame & Guilt feelings:

_____

So, we have two parts of the victim cycle. We have received the bad behavior and our inner critic took over our minds with shame and guilt. The inner child is suddenly shrinking in pain from our past and though we become fearful. This process is a pattern we remember and on some level are familiar with. We do not speak up for ourselves, we do not know how to enforce boundaries or even what those boundaries should look like, and the bad behavior is internalized.

Now we have our inner nurturer that wants to make everything better. The natural response is to see the person that hurt us with greater power and validate the inner voices of shame. We excuse the bad behavior, internalize the pain, and begin "fixing" the person who caused the pain ignoring our own hurt. Now, if this seems familiar write down the justification you would tell yourself excusing the bad behavior and ignoring your inner self.

Justification:

_____

_____

These justifications are very scary because these rationalizations for receiving abuse can be entangled with all kinds of core beliefs. We can tell ourselves that love hurts, relationships tolerate problems, and faith requires sacrificial pain. You may have several reasons that seem reasonable at the time keeping you in a position to internalize pain like a slow poison. We may even believe that we deserve this treatment or worse, we may not even notice it is happening.

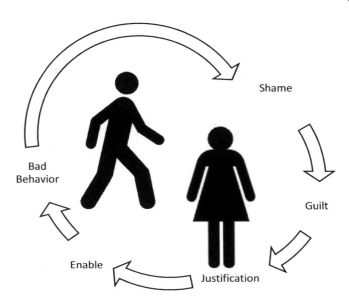

We move through our shame, guilt, and justification. We now become party to the cycle and enable the behavior to continue. This is the point in which bad behavior begins escalating into abuse. Toxic relationships exploit this process to inflict power and control. As you have filled out each of the previous lessons you have touched on each part of this cycle. We often look back at our lives and wonder how we could have tolerated so much. I know I did. I had no idea how I had wound up in the cycle I was in. But the biggest realization was how I was so comfortable with this cycle that I was essentially abusing myself by seeking out ways to keep the abuse in my life. I was a victim and I was my own abuser. By staying in my shame and guilt I was allowing the abuse. I was enabling it. I was setting up my relationships for failure so that I could stay in a cycle that was "comfortable". I had made my own cage and fashioned it after a cycle I had learned as a child based on a wounded inner self.

Recognizing this cycle is catalyst for change. Once you can see how your actions are keeping you in toxic cycles then you can begin to change. The other part of this realization is that you begin to understand how you cannot rescue someone in a victim cycle since they play such a huge part of the process and in turn you cannot be rescued. Until you are ready to leave the cycle you will repeat it or return to it. The other interesting fact to note is this cycle is not specific to women. Men can also receive and internalize abuse. Both individuals in the cycle share in the responsibility for change. Looking at this picture of the abuse cycle, take note of what role you play. How are you perpetuating pain and trauma in your life? You entered the cycle as a victim and through the process of engaging in your shame, guilt, and justification you never left the cycle. Isn't it time to leave it?

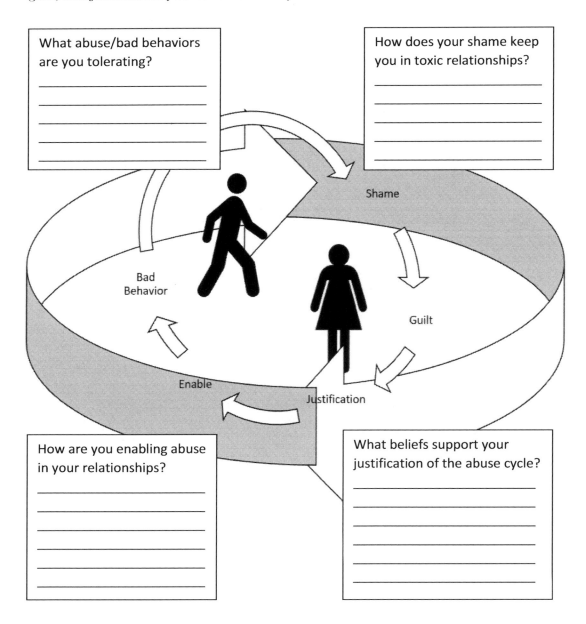

What abuse/bad behaviors are you tolerating?
_____
_____
_____
_____

How does your shame keep you in toxic relationships?
_____
_____
_____
_____

Shame

Bad Behavior

Guilt

Enable

Justification

How are you enabling abuse in your relationships?
_____
_____
_____
_____
_____

What beliefs support your justification of the abuse cycle?
_____
_____
_____
_____
_____

As you begin to understand the cycles you are in and how your internal processes play a huge role in your life you can begin to break the cycle. By changing the internal shame and justification process in your toxic relationships you can change your response. We can't change people, but we can change what we allow in our lives. By not playing a role in your abuse, by removing toxic behaviors, by rewriting the record of shame and guilt you can make steps to leave toxic relationships and cultivate the life you want.

Additional thoughts:

_____

_____

_____

_____

_____

_____

_____

_____

_____

Essential Oil and Grounding Intervention:

Cardamom

One of the best spices makes the beautiful oil Cardamom. Cardamom makes an excellent addition to any cup of hot tea or baked goods, but did you know that Cardamom helps with building feelings of security. In lesson one we learned the importance of security to our individual development. Most of our negative patterns are built on the compromise of our emotional security. Begin to cultivate feelings of security through meditation.

Using the cupping method apply one drop of cardamom and allow yourself to breathe deeply. Close your eyes and allow your mind drift to a place of complete comfort and safety. Picture what it looks like to be completely secure, accepted and loved. Allow yourself to sit in this feeling, allow it to wash over you. Think of this feeling as inside of your mind and body. If you find yourself distracted don't get discouraged, simply thank your brain for the interruption and return to your meditation. Notice your mind and body sensations, where you feel this sensation and allow the sensation of comfort to grow from a place inside of yourself.

These feelings are completely self-generated and from deep within you. As you let doubt, fear, and worry slip away you allow the meditation of security to grow within yourself. Dwell in this internal space of comfort. Breathe in and breathe out, use movements to pull strength into your meditation and stay completely connected to your internal security, your internal sense of self.

Each day that you meditate you will want to expand the time in which you can meditate working up to at least 12 minutes or more.

Date: _____

Meditation Length: _____

Date: _____

Meditation Length: _____

Date: _____

Meditation Length: _____

Date: _____

Meditation Length: _____

Additional thoughts:

_____

_____

_____

_____

_____

Writing Our Trauma Narrative

You have completed 7 lessons delving into the deep recesses of your past, pain, and patterns. You have learned so much about yourself. I am so proud of the work you are doing and all the changes you are primed to make at this point in your journey. Each lesson has included worksheets and note sections to help you recall some of your deepest trauma memories. To move forward in healing, it is important to create what is called a trauma narrative.

As we learned in lesson 2 about the brain rewiring information through a trauma lens, the way to heal is to untangle the trauma. To close the first section of the book you will write your trauma story. Everything you have had to overcome in each lesson of this section. It is important to recognize the pain and suffering without minimizing it. We want to focus on our strengths and our ability to overcome our hurts but be careful not to ignore the gravity of those hurts.

"The deeper that sorrow carves into your being, the more joy you can contain."

–Khalil Gibran

Take a moment to use an essential oil and ground yourself. Focus on your internal strength that has brought you through each lesson in this book. Are you ready to take this step towards healing together? Reviewing the memories you have recalled throughout the book, begin with your earliest memory and write each one down. Do your best to recall everything you can.

My Trauma Story:

_____

_____

_____

_____

_____

_____

_____

_____

Section 2: Identity

Reflection 8: Moving from Negative to Neutral

I want to welcome you to the next section of your journey. Remember that an object in motion stays in motion until met with an equal or opposite force. To reverse the cycle of trauma you will have to generate enough force to overcome every obstacle you have faced. Keep moving forward, you're doing great!

One of the hardest lessons I had to learn and sometimes still struggle with, is learning patience towards my healing journey. I remember my own journey through healing, I was so lost in my pain and sadness, and it is hard to notice the blessings in life when you live in a modern-day war zone. I remember the steps I took towards healing and how each step seemed more exhausting than the last, but it was these small decisions that lead to huge breakthroughs. This journey towards healing has taught me so much about myself. I wanted so badly to just skip over the painful memories and ignore the part I was playing in my trauma, but life does not operate on a predictable timeline and healing is not linear.

While development is on a standard time line, emotional healing isn't something that can be easily measured. Even physical recovery from injury is subject to the individual's pace and ability to heal. Learning to embrace your own pace of healing is one of the lessons I wished I had learned early in my journey. I spent so much time degrading myself for what I felt was a lack of adequate progress. I was ready to "get over" my dark emotions and I expected myself to simply be "better". I was intolerant to myself for my difficult feelings, for the exhaustion and compassion fatigue towards myself. I had moments of doubting every decision I had made in rebuilding my life. What had never occurred to me is that rehabilitation is painful, slow, and sometimes ugly yet so worth the freedom on the other side.

Setting expectations in healing is an important step for the beginning of the healing process. It can be very discouraging when you aren't seeing the progress you expect or feel that you will never reach a place of peace. The last thing that you need is to start working on building the life you want and sabotage your process through self-defeating behaviors or thoughts. We all want to be that super positive person that we all know who never seems to deal with situations realistically. You know the one I am talking about, every post on social media is some inspirational quote or uplifting statement. We all want to be that person and we beat ourselves up for not handling our pain so gracefully. "No, I don't feel like praying for that person today!" and "I don't think God even noticed that I stopped handling this well, a long time ago" and "I can just practice imagining my life is going to get better but at some point when I open my eyes it still feels like it is falling apart".

It is so hard to go through each of these very painful steps, feel and heal each memory, and put on a positive smile for the world. I don't know about you, but I didn't handle my chaos well. I just couldn't do it. So many told me "you just need to let go and let God". And I believe that is good advice but like any kind of advice, if it was that easy then I wouldn't be in the mess I was in to start with. Go from a negative mindset to being positive, it would have been easier to walk across Niagara Falls.

When setting expectations for rebuilding an authentic life, the goal isn't to go from negative to positive. That is a lot like going from third gear to reverse in a car. In trauma healing and recovery, the outcome of fast paced "quick fix" care will be similar to throwing out your transmission. The goal for any individual identity work is to move slowly through the process to give yourself time to overcome each negative pattern and create new lasting responses. Moving from negative to less negative, to neutral and then more positive, and finally positive. Setting a meaningful and realistic pace for healing can prevent you from feeling discouraged during difficult times.

One of the object lessons that helps drive this lesson home is orchids. I love to grow orchids in my home. Orchids have the most beautiful blooms, but they don't bloom year around. We can get discouraged when we don't see blooms in our life, but the reality is the greatest growth for an orchid is when it is growing deep strong roots. You won't always see beauty in your healing process, but that might be the time you are doing your deepest growth.

The truth is that as we work through our trauma and healing we will have to revisit these expectations and goals for our healing. It is a building block process but sometimes we must go back and rework lessons when we have things creep up and touch our old wounds. Learning to be kind to yourself in each season of your journey is critical for not reinjuring yourself with abusive thinking. As you begin to create a new narrative for your life it is important to begin this process with the relationship you have with yourself first. Take a few moments to list your expectations for yourself. Answer the questions below and consider what progress would be meaningful to you.

What things/relationships/habits do I not want in my life after healing?

_____

_____

_____

What challenges to healing do you face?

_____

_____

_____

How will I create support my healing journey?

_____

_____

_____

What relationships support my healing process?

_____

_____

_____

What physical symptoms do you want freedom from?

_____

_____

_____

What part of my personality do I want to manage better?

_____

_____

_____

How will I know that I am getting better?

_____

_____

_____

Finally write the length of time you have spent in the abuse cycle _____.
Now allow yourself the same amount of time to find healing and peace from the
trauma. It may or may not take that long but setting reasonable expectations is
crucial.

Write your short-term expectations below and the projected date you plan to revisit
your goals. Write down the results you are looking for in every stage of your
growth. Negative to less negative, to neutral, to more positive and finally living a life
in positivity. The neutral zone is an important position in the healing process. It can
be built into someone's life as a safety net for growth and for setbacks. If you find
yourself moving forward into positive healing but get set back rely on this neutral
zone for rest and support.

In the Negative column write commitments that will help you remove negativity (i.e.
set limits on time with toxic relationships, turn off music that reminds me of old
behaviors or patterns, stop bringing work home that prevents me from being fully
connected to my family). In the neutral column add commitments that are realistic
to maintaining a position of rest (i.e. I will spend time every week practicing yoga or
going to the gym, I will give myself 7-8 hours of sleep every night, I will not add
complex goals like weight loss while focusing on my pain). In the Positive column
add goals for a new lifestyle of wellness (i.e. I will begin building positive
relationships, I will work on a bucket list).

There might not be enough lines in this graph so use the space provided for notes.
Include a review date so you can come back and check on your expectations.
Remembering to always be gentle with yourself in the process. When setting a time
from for healing you want to consider the length of time you have spent in injury
and give yourself equal time to heal. How will you move your life gently towards a
more positive direction?

Consider the various obstacles that can affect your recovery time. One of the main reasons it is important to place relationships on hold during a healing process is that relationships add layers of expectations to our journeys. Consider the various relationships that might need to be adjusted during the healing process and how you can build in support for yourself. An honest conversation about placing their expectations on a lower priority level may be important.

Negative:
1._____
_____
2._____
_____
3._____
_____
Revisit Date:
_____

Neutral:
1._____
_____
2._____
_____
3._____
_____
Revisit Date:
_____

Positive:
1._____
_____
_____
2._____
_____
3._____
_____
Revisit Date:
_____

Additional thoughts:

_____

_____

Essential Oil and Grounding Intervention:

Rosemary

Self-sabotage is a very real concept for individuals working towards personal growth. The brain is hard wired to feel comfortable and learning to grow as a person can bring to surface fear and vulnerability. The essential oil Rosemary helps address feelings of sabotage. As you step away from past cycles of pain you may find new behaviors difficult and fear of success may affect your ability to focus on your journey. Learning to rest as you grow will help you maintain the process. In this activity we will use cupping or diffusing Rosemary and engaging in meditation. Close your eyes and focus on your deep breathing. Imagine an ocean washing over your fears slowly pulling each grain of sand from the shore. Breathe in and out and with each breath, picture your worry slip away. Spend several minutes naming your fears and allow them to drift with the tide as you release your fears begin to feel your heart lighten and turn your mind rest.

Rest allows you to be fully present and open for every experience. Rest allows you to be grounded in your choices. Rest allows your mind to focus on what is important, the new life you are creating. Rest, breathe, and allow you fears to slip away. Rub your palms on the back of your neck at the base of your skull and allow the oils to stay with you throughout the day.

Identity

Reflection 9: Noticing Ourselves Again

In the last several chapters we have focused everything that has hurt you. Life is filled with moments of suffering and difficulties. So how do we move beyond the pain? How do we begin to learn how to love ourselves again? Now that I know what I don't want in my life, what is it that I want? Who do I want to be? This is a much harder question to answer than most people realize. This is possibly one of the most important questions of your life, so let's take some time to really analyze this. I read a study once that said women begin forming their personal identity around the age of 25 years. I found in my experience the years 26-30 were when I decided who I did not want to be.

At 30 I had taken one of the greatest risks of my life and began restoring relationships that I had thought we lost to me. At 31 I was on my way to knowing a new-found purpose and strength as a woman, mother, wife, and friend. The years after were not easier and have been filled with difficulties and challenges. Restoration of self does not include a hardship free guarantee. I will say that because of the work I have done to support my own process I have been able to stay grounded in the person I decided to be. When I find myself doubting I simply look back on my journey. I know who I choose to be and why I choose this person, me.

In neuropsychology the brain is outlined as being two separate and connected entities. There is the actual brain. The way it functions and how it works. This is the brain you were given organically and biologically. This part of your brain stops developing at about 25 years old. This is the brain that is affected by sleep, diet, medication, and stress. The other part of your brain is called the brain self. This is the collection of memories, feelings, experiences, and identity. This part of the brain is responsible for the thoughts you think. This is your identity. This part of the brain can be affected by your relationships, choices, and beliefs.

The interesting thing about the brain is, both parts of your brain are profoundly affected by your environment, but the brain self can become disconnected with the organic brain. The environment that cultivates abuse profoundly impacts how you process information organically and how that information is used to define who you are. If you use avoidance and numbing as coping strategies for trauma a disconnect between the brain's self and organic brain is created.

So, ask yourself again, now that you know what you don't want, what do you want in your environment that supports your healing, both your organic brain but also your identity? Start with a simple exercise, noticing. Take time every day to just notice yourself in every activity you do. I started with how I drink coffee. I loved the taste of good coffee and I started developing a specific method for how I drank my coffee and focused on the small rhythms of enjoying coffee daily. I also set up small behavioral patterns that reminded me to notice myself and take moments of joy from the experience. I began to embrace the type of music I listened to as part of my identity. The way I cleaned my house. The small idiosyncrasies and ticks of my life that made me completely unique. Things that I noticed that perhaps no one else even knew about me. I opened my heart up to fall in love with myself.

Begin your list. Sometimes it is hard to start at the things we love about ourselves, so let's start with just the things we notice. You should try very hard to fill every line in these lists and even use additional note spaces. Challenge yourself to notice as much about you as possible over the next few days. Give yourself the permission to NOT question why you love or appreciate something but simply notice that sense of gratitude and self-pride.

What is it that you notice about yourself?

_____

_____

_____

_____

_____

_____

_____

_____

As you notice each part of your life, who you are, and the areas of your life you want to cultivate, remain open to appreciation for yourself. Remember that it is you that has brought yourself to this very moment. You have survived your very darkest days and created the very brightest of your memories.

We fall out of love with ourselves when we forget to remember who we truly are and move through life without thought. As you continue to recognize yourself be aware of what you would like more of in your life.

What is it that you want MORE of in your life?

_____

_____

_____

_____

_____

_____

_____

_____

Now focus on what you feel that you already have inside of you. Things about you that you truly love about yourself. This exercise may be difficult and if it is simply notice that it was difficult for you to answer this honestly. Push yourself to really answer it though. Keep in mind that you are perfectly designed with a complete purpose and plan for your life. Remind yourself of the one that created you and knows you by name. We may struggle for positive self-regard but our higher power delights in His creation.

What is it that you LOVE about yourself?

_____

_____

_____

_____

_____

Additional thoughts:

Essential Oil and Grounding Intervention:

Copaiba

Copaiba is a very soft oil with very strong capabilities. Copaiba essential oil supports a sense of wholeness, a feeling of being enough. This is a difficult concept in a woman's life and most women I know walk in a sense of lacking. To live authentically challenges the very concept of scarcity or not being or having enough. The idea that you have everything inside of you that you need to life a fulfilling and empowered life shuts down all self-doubt embedded in this idea that somehow you might be missing a critical part to your wholeness.

Take a drop of copaiba essential oil in your palm and breathe it in. Using the lesson of "Noticing" yourself, close your eyes and begin noticing how you feel about the word "enough". Begin meditating on the word "enough" and when you feel this sense of being enough. Notice I didn't say the word "abundance", just "enough". If this is a struggle for you simply take notice, it may be challenging at first. Breathe in and imagine enough air, imagine enough peace, imagine enough joy. Begin to invite a sense of enough-ness into your being and allow this idea to dwell in your heart. You are not incomplete, not when you cultivate truth mentally, physically, and spiritually that you are enough.

Additional thoughts:

_____

_____

_____

_____

_____

_____

_____

_____

_____

_____

_____

_____

_____

_____

_____

_____

_____

_____

_____

_____

_____

_____

Identity

Reflection 10: Beginning with Our Name

I love the story of Moses on the mountain with God. Do you know that story? Moses goes into the mountain and there he receives his calling, his important mission, and his BIG work! I wish sometimes God would just come down and slap us in the face with a burning bush! Wake up! You have a job to do! I think about how Moses grew up in trauma. Living as an outsider in the Pharaoh's house. It must have felt so isolating and then to be cast out to die. Talk about abandonment issues.

I was looking at the story of Moses in one of my Tuesday women's classes and something occurred to me about that time Moses spent in the house of his father-in-law. Moses was healing from trauma. You see his father in law was a priest who taught Moses of God. He gave him a trade and brought him into his family. This was the time of healing for Moses. I can only imagine the internal work Moses did during these years in Jethro's tents. And then God calls on Moses by name. This is the part that astounds me. God knows his name, and not just his name but all our names. Our names are so very powerful, they are a core pillar of our identity.

Moses didn't even know the name of God, in fact he says, "Who shall I say has sent me?" And God says, "I am, tell them "I am" has sent you". Here is the part that blew me away. Did you realize that EVERY time you introduce yourself as a person or as a description you are referring to God? I say, "I am Tara" and immediately I am attaching the identity of my higher power to my identity. The image of God in front of the image of me. Of course, I also say things like "I am fat" and "I am so stupid".

Horrible things to attach to my identity and to the identity of my God. Maybe God is fat but I kind of doubt it. The point is that the things we call ourselves are deeply rooted in our self-concept beyond just our thoughts and feelings about ourselves. They attach themselves to our core values and faith. I believe that if you want to know who you are you first must find out what it is you are calling yourself.

There is a catch to this lesson, our names have purpose attached to them, and we must walk in that purpose as Moses did. We are not always going to be excited about who we are, just as Moses came up with some pretty great excuses to not live up to his name. It is important to understand both the light and darkness about our identity. Let me explain. My name means Tower. When I think of a tower I first thought of strength but the more I meditated on what my name meant the more I realized the various implications to the meaning of tower.

A tower was a sign of civilization, a strong hold for war, a place to hold princesses' captive. A tower may be home to a dragon or used as a place of torture. A tower could be anything and everything described. I began to draw out how this idea of a tower describe the many facets of who I felt that I was. I was all those things. I was incredibly strong, a place of protection engineered to withstand outside attacks. I also had great fear in my life and internally tortured myself in darkness. I felt that inside of myself there was that inner child who felt she was a princess lost in time. I drew an incredible story just from my name and I loved every part of this imagination play. I felt incredible and I was very proud of the tower I was and had become.

I love to google "meaning of _____ name" and look for the top three origins or meanings. You can try websites such as Baby Names, Behind the Name, or The Baby Name Wizard. Write the meaning and origin of your names:

First name:

_____

Middle name:

_____

Last name:

_____

Now draw a picture of how the meaning of your name describes you:

Write your "I am" statements. List some of the descriptions you refer to yourself.

_____

_____

_____

_____

What do you notice about these statements? Do you think that these statements help or hinder your living in your true purpose? How does your name tie into your identity and your life purpose?

Additional thoughts:

_____

_____

_____

_____

_____

_____

_____

_____

Essential Oil and Grounding Intervention:

Hyssop

For this grounding intervention we will use Hyssop. I love Hyssop for its ability to support the body's wellness, but it is important to note straight off that Hyssop can elevate blood pressure if you are experiencing high blood pressure. You may want to begin with just one drop and be mindful of how you feel and experience the oil. For emotional support Hyssop heightens a person's self-awareness and is one of my favorites.

Because of Hyssops powerful health properties. I like to diffuse hyssop or apply it topically over my heart. As you are focused on increasing your self-awareness I want you to turn your mind towards rhythms. Because of the way the brain develops, rhythmic motions help calm the mind and reduces a sense of anxiety. This is why the ocean is so relaxing, rocking back and forth, much like listening to music.

This is also why women often find cleaning therapeutic, the gentle rhythms of vacuuming and washing dishes or folding clothes helps calm the mind and bring peace, plus your house is clean in the end. Even eating some foods can become rhythmic in nature. To calm the mind and allow yourself to engage each part of your life it is time to notice the rhythmic patterns you are mind-numb to. Begin to practice healthy rhythmic patterns that help cultivate your sense of autonomy rather than numb your awareness.

Breathe in your oil and begin rocking your body from side to side. Breathe in and out as you just gently sway allow your mind to be at peace. Notice how it feels to move in this direction. Allow your sense of self to grow as you focus on each joint that moves, each muscle that stretches and each sway of your body. Notice your internal process and slow down your mind. Breathe and be fully present in your body and mind.

Identity

Reflection 11: Creating a New Self-Identity

I think most women in their life at some point feel lost, that they just aren't good enough or the work they do will never be appreciated. Do you know what it feels like to be constantly chasing the sensation of acceptance? This was me. I always knew I could do anything I set my mind to. I took great pride in my ability to set my mind to a new task and learn a new skill. I am hardworking and die hard when it comes to breaking limitations. But the problem was that I didn't feel loved or accepted for WHO I was, just what I did. I built my relationships on what I could do for other people and not the joy or happiness I brought to their life.

In fact, I couldn't even imagine someone finding joy with me if I wasn't performing some level of service for them. Even my faith was built on my need to justify my life through works. There was no room for grace. All the stuff we processed in the trauma section of this book was affecting how I viewed my self-worth and value. This imbalance of self-identity was creating suffering in myself that poured over into my relationships. It wasn't until I started unpacking my self-identity and really looking at my self-worth that I began to see how to work on this.

Self-identity is made up of two parts. Self-efficacy which is the value a person places on their ability to do things, overcome challenges, and perform well when faced with obstacles. Self-esteem is the value a person finds in their existence as they are. This could be in reference to their physical characteristics or their personality, the knowledge that who they are brings value to the world. Self-esteem and self-efficacy are two parts to a balanced self-image. If you have a strong sense of your personal worth but don't do things of value to move your life forward in a positive direction than you will suffer, and your relationships will suffer too. If you have an over compensating tendency to take on more tasks and more achievements but doubt your value and believe that you don't matter to the people in your life, then you will suffer, and your relationships will suffer. You are a human-BEING and not a human-DOING. I have found that many women struggle with one side of their self-identity. They put all their value in the part that comes naturally. The secret is balance.

In the last couple of lessons you have been looking at the habits in your life that create your sense of self. The coffee your drink, music you listen to, the names you call yourself. You have an outline of your identity.

When you think of yourself what do you tell others about you?

_____

_____

_____

Look at what you wrote down. Did you list titles, descriptive words, character qualities, or attributes? Let's break this down even further.

Describe yourself (physical appearance):

_____

_____

_____

List your unique attributes (personality, special features, and abilities):

_____

_____

_____

List your titles (achievements, status, relationship markers):

_____

_____

_____

Write about your character (qualities and inadequacies):

_____

_____

_____

Esteem: Being	Efficacy: Doing

The next question is whether it is balanced in both self-esteem and self-efficacy. Look back on the patterns of beliefs and ideas that shape you. Are they DOING patterns or BEING patterns? For each of the questions you filled out above analyze if they have value because it is something you do or something you are? Action verses existence. Fill in the columns of descriptions and attributes, personalities and characters that fit as either Self-esteem or Self-efficacy. The important part of this process is not to judge where you are at with your self-identity. Not to feel bad or good about yourself. Simply to look at where you are at with your thoughts and feelings. Do your thought patterns about yourself help or hinder you from your healing? Loving ourselves begins with knowing ourselves. Understanding who we are and how we can grow.

What things do you notice that you would like to grow about your self-identity?

_____

_____

_____

Additional thoughts:

_____

_____

_____

_____

_____

_____

_____

_____

_____

_____

_____

_____

_____

_____

_____

_____

Essential Oil and Grounding Intervention:

Geranium

When we spend time in sadness and walking a life where we feel that we are only reacting we can become engulfed in the disappointment, we can lose our sense of self-direction and purpose. One of the most important parts of reclaiming our future is to connect to our life vision. The difference between being emotionally stuck and simply struggling in a difficult season is the power of vision. Those that are emotionally stuck cannot see the role that their feelings and behaviors play in repeating the same patterns in their lives.

Those that are in difficult seasons can struggle with the same feelings, but they understand that they will not stay in this season, their life has a vision and they will continue to work towards their purpose even in difficulty. If you have never spent time pondering your life purpose and vision then it might be difficult to answer the questions in this section of the book, but it is the perfect time to begin.

Using Geranium essential oil in the cupping method we have practiced I want you to focus your mind's eye in a meditation. Our life can be a lot like driving a bus, close your eyes, breathe in and imagine you are driving a bus. You have a set route, a schedule, and passengers in your life but YOU are the driver. Take a few moments to consider the condition of your bus. Think about the maintenance it might need, if you have gas in your tank, if you have an engine in good repair. Breathe.

Picture your passengers and any conversations you might need to have with them in supporting you having a positive driving experience on this road of life. Now take hold of the wheel of your bus and imagine where you will drive your life. Where are you heading? Are you taking the same route with a few changes in stops or are you turning a new direction? Lay out a map in your mind and allow yourself to feel the freedom of these changes. You are establishing a vision for your "life bus".

Keep your mind focused on how by taking care of your bus and having the right passengers you can keep your bus moving in a positive direction towards a route that brings meaning to your life. Buses don't have the ability to make sharp turns so be gentle with yourself and remember gradual changes in a positive direction will be easier to handle and won't crash the bus. Breathe in and breathe out and keep this beautiful oil with you throughout the day. You might be driving a Struggle Bus or the Hot Mess Express, but you are going in the direction of your heart.

Additional thoughts:

_____

_____

_____

_____

_____

_____

_____

_____

_____

_____

_____

_____

_____

_____

_____

_____

_____

_____

_____

_____

_____

_____

_____

Identity

Reflection 12: Even Gardens Have Fences

I have a garden, a garden that has quickly grown into a hobby farm. I love the process of watching things grow. Working hard with your hands and putting your time, knowledge and effort into something that brings life. There are many therapeutic lessons I have learned and shared through my adventures gardening. One day in my Tuesday class the women asked me to teach on boundaries. How does someone who has never been good at keeping relationships healthy and supportive suddenly set boundaries? I think this is a very important question in healing. Setting boundaries is such a vague concept. What does it actually mean to have boundaries and how do you reset your relationships to support and maintain boundaries? It is all so confusing, so we started talking about gardening.

Healing trauma is the same process as cultivating a garden from an unloved plot of land. You must spend time getting to know the sun's patterns over the garden, the way the wind blows, the type of soil and what it needs to be rested and ready for planting. You begin to clear every plant, weed, rock, or root that isn't wanted in the new garden. This takes time and sometimes you do this in small sections at a time. I usually draw up plans for my garden and research the seeds and growing patterns for the food I want to produce. I spend time learning about this space I am preparing to grow in and then I begin to set up a fence. The first year I didn't build a fence around my garden and just as I was seeing true growth in my vegetable patch, a large blue tractor driven by my husband clipped the corner of my boxes and flung the entire frame into the air destroying my patch. I was devastated. You see, I had not built a fence to separate my garden from the lawn and it cost me that whole season's investment, the time, money, and hopes of a good harvest.

Fences for gardens are like boundaries for relationships. You have taken the time to work on removing all the painful hurt in your life and prepared your heart for healing. You have been learning about yourself and you are becoming open to the idea of growing your life again. The last thing you need is for a garden destroying rodent or unsuspecting tractor driver to find its way in and plow over your hard work. You have worked so hard to be at this point in your journey the next question is not how defensive you will be but how will you protect yourself while growing your life, so you can have a harvest to share. In this exercise we will start working on a plan for a growing space. It is important to set the expectation that when gardening for the first time to begin on a manageable scale and limit yourself to what you know to start. The same is true with healing. In the chart below fill out your healing garden. Ask yourself what would you like to grow in your life? What do you plan to enjoy and how will you nurture and care for your garden? What kind of fence would you have? Draw and design a depiction of how you see your own healing journey.

My Healing		
Hope	Love	Respect
_____	_____	_____
_____	_____	_____
_____	_____	_____

Gate

Now that you have a clear idea of your healing design ask yourself a few questions. It is important to understand what we are growing and who we are growing with? What kind of people that we have around us as be able to cultivate this growth. The importance of boundaries comes in to play when we start involving others in our process. Think of the people in your life. Who belongs in your garden, who belongs on the outside of your garden? Who will you share your harvest with and who will you not?

Now that you have worked so hard to build a beautiful garden is there anyone you trust to toil along-side of you in your garden helping you grow?

_____

Is anyone currently in your life that is destroying your garden?

_____

Do you have people that ignore your fence and help themselves to your "vegetables"?

_____

Do you have onlookers like buzzards over your fence mocking your plans, if so, who?

_____

Do you know anyone that would gladly take what you have grown but refuse to grow their own life?

_____

Add the answers to these questions to your drawing as a visual reminder of setting up boundaries in these relationships.

Spend some more time thinking on your garden as if it was your healing heart. Who do you keep inside your gentle growing space and who needs to stay on the outside of the gate? Your personal boundaries are not terrible things to reject people or hurt relationships. They are simply fencing to allow you to grow, enjoy, and share.

Write out your plan for setting up fences (boundaries) in your life:

_____

_____

_____

_____

_____

Additional thoughts:

_____

_____

_____

_____

_____

_____

_____

_____

_____

_____

_____

_____

Essential Oil and Grounding Intervention:

Lemongrass

When we begin to make changes in our lives one of our greatest mental hurdles to overcome is often our fear of judgement or criticism. We can project our own internal judgements onto situations and relationships or we can be vulnerable to other people's unkindness or opinions.

When you are learning new behaviors or changing old thinking patterns we can feel raw and exposed. Lemongrass is one of my favorite oils. It resonates with these feelings of fear of judgement and a sense of rawness. You can smell the wet grass and fresh life scent. Lemongrass is beautiful when diffused in the air and breathed in. I also use Lemongrass in my diet to help cleanse internally and support my body.

Take time to allow yourself to connect to your sense of raw growth and tenderness to your harsh environment. Keep your mind centered on the processes of seedlings forming roots. Before the roots are strong, the sprouts of young seedlings are vulnerable to the conditions. To strengthen seedling sprouts a gardener will set the tray of new growth outside during the day and bring them in at night to allow them to adapt to the environment. Limited exposure to the elements.

You are the young seedling and to always keep yourself protected from judgement will not prepare you to live in the environment of life. You must be mindful of limiting your exposure to harsh emotions but still allow yourself to be strengthen by the exposure. Use lemongrass to allow yourself to process the fears that are connected to experiencing judgement and stay mentally focused on the courage that comes from facing the things that we fear and staying open to life.

Additional thoughts:

_____

_____

_____

_____

_____

_____

_____

_____

_____

_____

_____

Identity

Reflection 13: Becoming Your Super Hero

I can only imagine how full your life is every day. If you are like me, your day is filled with huge adult decisions and tiny tasks woven with moments of uncertainty. So many responsibilities that if left undone the semi-succinct life you lead might crumble in minutes. I cleaned my house on Sunday, it took 4 hours and by Tuesday noon it was trashed again. I know as a mom and wife I can't turn my back on these people living in my home. Oh, I love them, but I can't trust them with a clean room. I cannot tell you how many times I wish for some version of super nanny to appear and magically change the flow of my life. If only I had a super power of my own to vanquish the chaos, rebuild my worn-down energy levels, or at least run through the school drop off lines in lightning speed. I hope I am not alone in this. I am over here singing Bonnie Tyler "Holding Out for a Hero" with some Konmari skills.

Heroes are powerful imaginations across cultures. We all have our heroes and we all know that one superpower we would have if only we had been dropped into a vat of radioactive acid or zapped with gamma rays. Like people suffering with trauma, super heroes also have very humble or even tragic beginnings. They are usually victims of pain or rejection, and I find the parallels to super heroes rather striking and perhaps that is why we gravitate to their stories. As a woman I think it is important to see what we value in our heroes. I wonder how many decisions I made still caught in my victim cycle that were based in an idea that a hero would save me from my own chaos. We recognize strength in others and deny our own inner power.

Think back to when you were a child, which super hero did you most admire? What were their strengths?

_____

_____

What did you value about this power?

_____

What was the influence this hero had because of their power?

_____

How were their human weaknesses turned into strengths?

_____

_____

Now, let's look a little closer at your healing journey through trauma. In the last couple of lessons, you are increasing your self-awareness and taking inventory of every part of your identity. You are outlining beliefs and value systems. You have opened your mind to new growth processes. You have left your abuse cycle and are changing your victim ideology. You are no longer that weak suffering person powerless over their fate. You are the brand-new super hero right after they have discovered their powers. You now get to design how you will use these powers and save your life.

What are your strengths?

_____

_____

_____

What is the influence you would like to have in your own life or relationships?

_____

_____

_____

What strengths have you developed because you have overcome your own weakness?

_____

_____

How are you working towards making your world a better and safer place?

_____

_____

_____

Now I want you to look back on the questions you answered about your own childhood super hero. What are the ties between your own journey and the superhero you admired?

_____

_____

_____

Many women that work through this exercise find that the super hero they valued as a child was the one with a power that they felt they needed to feel safe in their world at that time.

Spend some time thinking on yourself, how you are and have always been your own hero if you only stopped discounting your own inner power and embraced who you are. Many individuals are not able or willing to leave the abuse cycles in their life. Many dream of a rescuer but never imagine that they are the answer to their healing.

You alone hold the key to break the chains that bind you. You might not be able to adult well, you might struggle to get your kids to school on time, and you might not be able to save the world from laundry piles. But you can save yourself and that my friend is enough. Draw yourself as your own Super Hero:

I am my own Super Hero

Now take time to recognize how you have leveraged this internal strength, this super power within your own life. Take an honest assessment of your life and look for moments of success or achievement and find the internal power that helped you push through. What strength did you find inside yourself during these struggles?

Think of the strength it has taken to complete some of these worksheets and sift through these memories of pain or sadness. We become our true selves when we stop discounting and discrediting our inner powers and walk in our gifts. You already have the power you need to set yourself free, if only you would recognize it and allow yourself to operate in your internal power.

Additional thoughts:

_____

_____

_____

_____

_____

_____

_____

_____

_____

Essential Oil and Grounding Intervention:

Thyme

When we begin to rebuild our lives, we can struggle with feelings that often are new to us. If you notice your anxiety increasing when you focus on your self-work or in completing these activities let me assure you that this can be common. As you are increasing your mindfulness and learning to respond to your life differently you also need to learn to recognize and respond to your internal feelings differently. It is important for you to take time to put words to these feelings and turn your mind to connect these feelings to where they generate in your body.

As women, it can always be difficult to be fully aware of our bodies and emotions. Hormonal responses are sometimes uncontrollable. We can often sacrifice our health and diet to better accommodate other commitments. Thyme is an amazing oil for women, for balancing hormones and strengthening the body. The emotional affirmation with Thyme is "I will protect myself" and this is a powerful intention based on our lesson above. You have the strength to protect your emotional responses.

In this grounding exercise I would like us to do something a little different, to reconnect to our body through self-touch. One of the best methods for using thyme essential oils is in a massage along the spine and feet. Remember to test thyme on a small area of skin to test for sensitivity as it is herbaceous. Allow yourself to locate the feelings that are present in our mind and turn to our body and begin focusing on releasing the emotion.

Self-touch massages can be challenging but I love to focus on the reflexology points along the soles of my feet. Turning your self-judgement off and setting aside any hesitation to touch your own skin in an act of self-care, take each foot individually and dropping one drop of Thyme in your palm. You can dilute it with coconut oil if it creates any warming sensation on the skin.

Spend time focusing on each part of the bottom of your foot, focus on releasing pressure and quiet the mind during this exercise. You can practice this process with your hands, your scalp and any other part of your body where you can reach comfortably. Practice connecting with your body throughout the week and as you feel overwhelmed with changes or emotions turn your mind to the pain and take time to gently release it with massage.

Additional thoughts:

_____

_____

_____

_____

_____

_____

_____

_____

_____

Identity

Reflection 14: Balance is a 5

Super hero woman that you are, let's jump into the last lesson of section two. Today we will learn about balance. We have covered so many great lessons and you are making huge progress in your journey. Now we will learn how to set daily expectations for your next steps in this journey. Of course we want to apply every lesson we learn and every tool we pick up. We want to transform our lives, our family relationships, and our careers. We want to be the Pinterest mom with Instagram worthy photos of our perfect lives but that just isn't going to happen every day.

We will have days where we are amazing mothers, wives, friends, and women and we will have days when we are captain of the Hot Mess Express driving our Struggle Bus filled with our bratty children. The same is true of trauma healing. We will have days where we are using our oils and grounding our mind and spirit. We will remember mindfulness and might even get a meditation session into our busy schedule. And then we will also have days where we are triggered with memories and held captive by our emotions in that moment.

Self-awareness is the key to understanding our trauma symptoms and how the cycles that held us hostage can still affect our daily lives. In therapy, journaling can be a powerful tool to keeping the mind focused on self-awareness. I like to help clients build and complete mood charts as part of their journaling process. A mood chart is a mental health tracker that is built around specific questions to help clients understand their personal baseline for wellness. To create a personal mood chart or mental health tracker you need to ask yourself what symptoms you would like to monitor and how those symptoms create complex issues for your wellness. There are a few important questions you can ask to help sort out what would be helpful to track.

What physical markers of trauma or other mental health symptoms do you experience?

_____

_____

What do you need physically to help balance your wellness? (i.e. sleep, nutrition, exercise)

What are the thought patterns that contribute to triggering your symptoms?

 What are the relationships that impact your wellness and what goals are you working on in these relationships?

What do you notice about experiences that trigger your symptoms?

To chart this into data I usually recommend a number line or graph system. I created an example for you but there are many ways to create mood charts. The most important part is to select the appropriate information that will support your healing. Sleep, mood, pace of thought, and appetite are basic information to begin tracking, combined with one or two specific goals for your wellness. Your individual goals can be outlined from past lessons or from your work with a counselor. Write down at least two personal goals you are working on and would like to track the results.

Goal 1:

_____

_____

_____

Goal 2:

_____

_____

_____

This mood chart marks 10 as representing the best score possible and the 1 representing the lowest. Remember your goal is balance. The three-day sample below can be used as a template and transferred into a journal. I keep my tracker in my planner and I recommend tracking your symptoms for 6 months to a year to get a complete understanding of your wellness cycles.

For those of you that are familiar with Excel spread sheets you can convert this information into all kinds of charts, but I like to simply look back over a month at a time and see if there are any patterns developing.

(See graphic on next page.)

Day 1

Hours of sleep

1 2 3 4 5 6 7 8 9 10

Mood

1 2 3 4 5 6 7 8 9 10

Appetite

1 2 3 4 5 6 7 8 9 10

Pace of Thoughts

1 2 3 4 5 6 7 8 9 10

Goal:_____

1 2 3 4 5 6 7 8 9 10

Goal:_____

1 2 3 4 5 6 7 8 9 10

Day 2

Hours of Sleep

1 2 3 4 5 6 7 8 9 10

Mood

1 2 3 4 5 6 7 8 9 10

Appetite

1 2 3 4 5 6 7 8 9 10

Pace of Thoughts

1 2 3 4 5 6 7 8 9 10

Goal:_____

1 2 3 4 5 6 7 8 9 10

Goal:_____

1 2 3 4 5 6 7 8 9 10

Day 3

Hours of sleep

1 2 3 4 5 6 7 8 9 10

Mood

1 2 3 4 5 6 7 8 9 10

Appetite

1 2 3 4 5 6 7 8 9 10

Pace of Thoughts

1 2 3 4 5 6 7 8 9 10

Goal:_____

1 2 3 4 5 6 7 8 9 10

Goal:_____

1 2 3 4 5 6 7 8 9 10

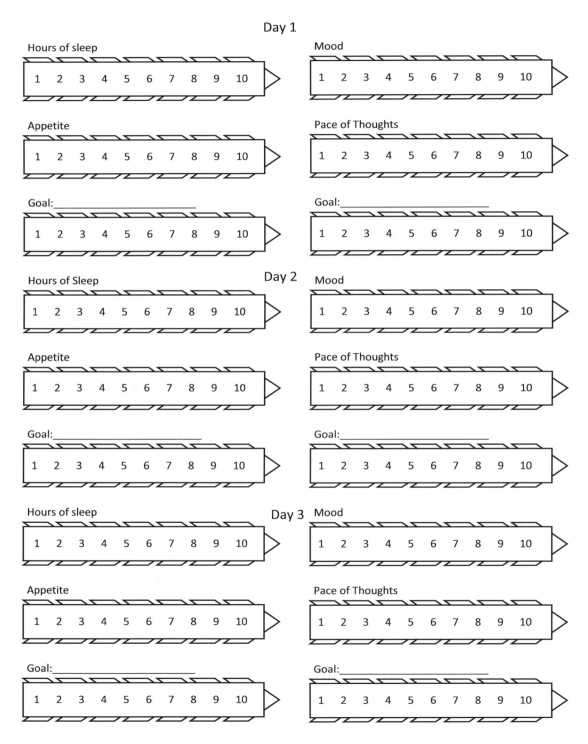

Once you have at least a month of data you should be able to look for patterns and even add notes of the factors that impacted the scores for the day. Remember this is just a sample and not a comprehensive list. You can track as many symptoms as you are working on at a time. Be mindful of stress, relationships, even whether can create waves in our healing process. Remember to also consider hormonal shifts or other medical or mental health conditions that can impact these numbers.

Now let's talk about your expectations. I know you will want to circle a 10 every day. I know you will want to rock every part of your recovery process but that is neither realistic nor healthy. People who are on 10 for more than a couple of days in a row may need to be checked for mania.

During the beginning stages of healing you should shoot to average around a 5. Leave room in your life to grow. If you can manage your wellness on an average level and show up to the life you have built everyday then you are winning. Focus your mind to be strength based when assessing your results. What areas are you experiencing success with and what things helped to you reach that success?

Notes:

_____

_____

_____

_____

_____

Additional thoughts:

_____

_____

_____

_____

_____

_____

Essential Oil and Grounding Intervention:

Basil

Self-work can be so challenging because unlike other type of effort it is hard to measure progress. In this lesson we learned a creative method for tracking progress, but the reality is that our emotional responses to our limitations can often sabotage our growth. We can get discouraged and give up on good work if we do not demonstrate an understanding for ourselves. Understanding is one of the greatest challenge relationships face and often we can focus this outwardly but not towards ourselves.

The essential oil Basil helps to increase a sense of understanding in the emotional mind. As you complete each of these lessons in this workbook you are asking yourself difficult questions to grow and strengthen your understanding of yourself. One of the fundamentals of understanding is learning to ask open questions and apply active listening. Active listening is when you listen with your body and mind. Too often our minds are so filled with thoughts and conclusions that we don't listen from a place of openness. When we listen to our own hearts we do the same thing, we are filled with distractions and excuses. Our sophistication and pride limit our ability to remain open to our inner desires.

In this exercise we will begin with diffusing basil and breathing in its strong scent. When I first diffused basil it gave me a strong headache and by blending it with other oils I was able to enjoy the benefits for opening my thoughts. With any of the oils that you struggle to enjoy you can blend them with a couple of drops of the oils you enjoy.

Breathe in and open your mind, focus on listening to your heart. What would your heart say if it knew you would understand? Be still, breathe, and listen. Allow your heart to generate answers to your invitation for understanding. Spend time each day listening to your heart and what it says. It may have different feelings and different thoughts each day.

Simply listen and seek to understand, do not put action into play. Sometimes our hearts will feel lost and cry out to give up on something that hurts, don't react but listen and allow your heart to know that you are listening. I hear you, I am here for you. I hear myself and I am here for myself. Remain open and stay connected to who you are as you move forward to the last section of this book.

Additional thoughts:

_____

_____

_____

_____

_____

_____

_____

_____

_____

_____

_____

_____

_____

_____

_____

_____

_____

_____

_____

_____

_____

_____

_____

_____

_____

Your Identity Narrative

Take a few moments to look back over the last 7 lessons you have completed. Your self-awareness has grown so much in these lessons. You should see yourself noticing more and more with each day. One of my favorite psychologists Jordan B. Peterson, PhD. said that a life spent learning about yourself is not a life wasted. I believe that this is one of the greatest strengths a person can have is to know each part of their soul and the imprints they leave on the world around them.

Take a few moments to think of all that you have learned about yourself and write down a whole picture of who you believe you are and how being you brings life value. Remember to embrace every part of your life. Your goodness and your chaos, your darkness and your joy, the fears and grace within you that brings light to your spirit. You are becoming your authentic self.

_____

_____

_____

_____

_____

_____

_____

_____

_____

_____

_____

_____

_____

Section 3: Commitments

Reflection 15: Commitment 1 -
When Self-love is Lost, Begin with Gratitude

Welcome to the last section of this journey towards your authentic life. This section focuses on the commitments you make to yourself that keep you growing and pursing your passion and purpose. When you started this journey, you held your pain in the center of your heart and kept yourself caged. Over the last few lessons you have begun to open your heart again and step out of your patterns that kept you trapped. Now we will strengthen each of these new choices to empower you to be in love with the life you have created.

I was in Hobby Lobby yesterday and saw a sign that said "I saw that"- God and I smiled to myself for a moment. The old me would have read that and felt conviction and judgement from my higher power but the authentic and free woman that I am today knows that when I am seen by my God he smiles with pride, shakes his head and laughs a little at my crazy mess. This is the message of grace that only comes when we walk in commitments of love for ourselves. Let's take these last few steps together. I want you to know this powerful experience of self-love.

When you hear the term self-love and self-care what comes to mind for you? For me this was so hard to even put these terms into practice. It sounded like just more tasks on my plate to come up with energy to complete. I would add things to my schedule that I truly enjoyed doing like go to the gym, get my nails done, spend time with friends but then my routine would change, life would get busy, or someone would get sick and I would be exhausted. So, one by one my lovely self-care plan would go to pots and I would feel like a failure for not doing the things that helped me not feel like a failure. I would look in the mirror and new negative narratives began to form.

The idea of loving myself seemed further and further from my reach. What I didn't realize was that with all the therapeutic work I had done to help myself heal I was still fighting against acceptance of myself. I was reading a book and something in the book sparked a simple thought on what was missing in my self-care plan. I wasn't even grateful for my body, my brain, or my personality. I had been so adjusted to trying to improve and get better than I had missed a critical step of appreciating myself.

Gratitude is a lost art in our culture. We live mindlessly moving through our lives and even when we start noticing our patterns we forget how precious our abilities are as we are the active agents in our own lives. I was being purposeful but discounted the power I had in my processes. As shame cannot survive empathy; love cannot exist without gratitude. I stopped and looked at my body, my life, and my journey and began to open my heart to the gratitude I have for all I have done and for who I am.

A self-care plan is built on the foundation of supporting our wellness on simple commitments to gratitude, acceptance, and compassion. We can fill our schedules and do many things we love but they can become as tedious as any activity if they are not built on the basic principles that grow love in our lives. The idea of gratitude can be a bit aloof. Gratitude to me is a larger concept than a simple "thank you", or "I am grateful for...". Gratitude is deeper recognition of value. Many people begin with a gratitude list and this is a good way to start noticing and exercising gratitude. I would challenge women to do this for themselves first.

Take time to look at yourself in a mirror. What is it that you see? What is it you feel? Is there anything that you feel gratitude for in your reflection? In everything you see what has brought meaning to your life? I see wrinkles and cellulite and scars at first when I look at myself. But then I see a body that has loved, touched, and held so many beautiful people, born life, and built dreams.

I might not always see "success" (what-ever that means) but I do see strength. I see value and meaning behind each part of who I am. If I look past the unsightly in the different areas of my life I can see the journey that brought me to this moment. There is a verse that says "How beautiful on the mountains are the feet of those that bring good news..." Isaiah 52:7. If you think about this, feet on the mountains means those feet have journeyed across traitorous terrain. I don't think they had Dr. Scholl's and pedicures in the Old Testament, so these feet must look like my body feels, a little worn from the journey. The one that carries the message of peace across mountains is you. You have carried peace in you and are made more beautiful from your journey.

On the left side of the chart below list the things you see in yourself that you have gratitude for. Your body, your mind, your personality, your soul, the things that you have noticed about yourself. You don't have to love every part of yourself, but you are beautiful and have value in the message you share. On the other side of the mountain write the "message of peace" you feel that you are carrying. The message of hope only you carry for the relationships that you cultivate. This is your commitments in your life that keeps you pursuing your true self. The self that is valued and treasured. As you overflow with gratitude for yourself you will be able to extend that gratitude for others.

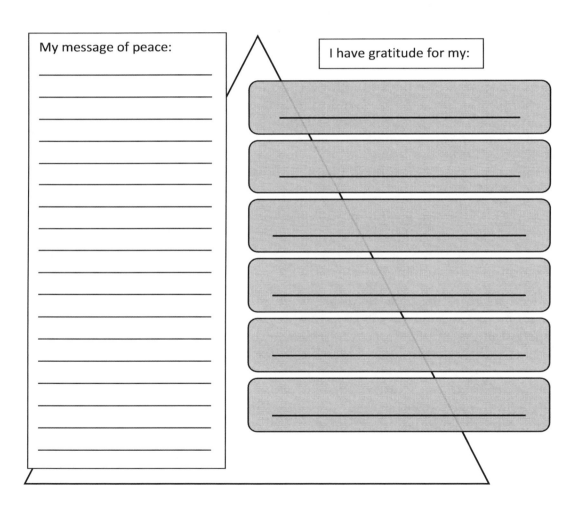

My message of peace:

I have gratitude for my:

Additional thoughts:

_____

_____

_____

_____

_____

_____

_____

_____

_____

_____

_____

_____

_____

_____

_____

_____

_____

_____

_____

_____

_____

_____

_____

Essential Oil and Grounding Intervention:

Peppermint

As we begin stepping into new behaviors and patterns of change we can move between feelings of motivation and fear. Each day begins with goal setting of small singular 5-degree changes towards wholehearted living. Peppermint essential oil activates the brain and energizes the mind in a way that encourages emotional growth. I enjoy peppermint diffused in the morning specifically to help energize my goal setting and morning mindset. The affirmation we use with peppermint is "I accept growth".

For this intervention we will rely on a more practical application of behavior change that will support new patterns. You don't have to change every part of your life at the same time. We have talked extensively about setting realist goals and supporting meaningful changes.

Sometimes we can allow the greatness of our calling to intimidate us from action. Our dreams can feel so big that they become unattainable. That is good, do not shy away from setting your goals higher than your abilities.

You already have everything you need to walk in the life you desire and as you work towards each step in your process you will continue to evolve your skills to reach your highest potential. Growth allows you to stretch your abilities and challenges your self-concept to become more than you knew possible.

With this exercise simply write down three small tasks each day this week that support your journey. Set up your diffuser and drop 3 drops of peppermint in. Breathe the refreshing aroma and allow your mind to engage in your plan to grow your self-love. Keep these tasks simple and connected to your personal vision for your life.

Some of my daily tasks include spending at least 5 minutes per day focused on a project or goal completely from my own creativity; reaching out to a friendship that is important to me; spending time being silent and practice listening to my heart; doing exercises that help me reduce physical pain and support my core strength; walking in my garden and praying through my prayer journal. You may want to look back at previous goals you set in other lessons for ideas on what might be meaningful for you.

Begin keeping track of your daily task list below:

_____

_____

_____

_____

_____

_____

_____

_____

_____

_____

_____

_____

_____

_____

_____

_____

_____

_____

_____

_____

_____

_____

_____

_____

Commitments

Reflection 16: Commitment 2 - Creating Acceptance by Giving Grace

It was difficult to decide the order of the last lesson and this one. Acceptance and gratitude are two of the core values to an authentic life. There is a concept in therapy called radical acceptance and that is the idea of accepting everything in life no matter how big or small. It is in our culture to have explanations for things that occur. We want to have answers to the questions "Why did this happen?" "What was the meaning?" "Why would God allow this?" but the reality is that we often do not know the answers to these questions and if we obsess over needing to know we can destroy our peace. We can prevent ourselves from healing because we want to have reasonable justification.

Beginning with total acceptance allows you to remove your need for control and preserve their inner peace. Sometimes it can seem simple to just move through life in acceptance but when the thing we struggle with is ourselves that can be a bit more complex. When we have early memories of rejection and abandonment then our sense of acceptance towards self can be broken. When we have not experienced acceptance in our early life we might not have a model for how this should look or feel. The goal of this book is not to minimize the lessons or your process but to provide a building block for you to grow.

For me understanding what acceptance would look like came from a movie scene. I had read many therapy books and was working through my psychology classes. I had spent many years working on my own healing journey and I felt that I still struggled reconciling my earliest memory of abandonment. This fear of abandonment would create insecurity in my relationships, my work, and my self-image. I wanted to "accept myself" but I did not know what that really meant. It was amazing to me that just through having a visual representation of acceptance from a movie I happened to watch, To the Bone, allowed me the peace and freedom to imagine the same compassion for myself.

I was able to meditate on that experience and though the person that had hurt me would never be able to recreate that for me, I could meet my own need and give that same love to myself. I could begin to accept myself. From this experience I have grown my self-acceptance. I have learned more about my own brain and personality. I speak of my strengths and limitations as building blocks for who I am. I also communicate and require that those who engage with me on a personal level understand what I need so that I can contribute to the relationship as my best self.

I visualize compassion for myself and how I can bring that compassion alive in actions towards myself and others. I treat myself a lot like you would your social media account. I try to capture everything in the most pleasant way possible and build on those strengths while being gentle with myself for my struggles. I spend time focused on what is working and going right in my life. I look at failures gently and even if I can't understand where I went wrong I practice resilience by not holding on to the pain and put the experience in the "one day this will make sense and be used to teach a lesson for someone" pile. With these simple methods of self-care and gratitude in my process I grow acceptance in my life.

For this exercise, imagine what self-acceptance would look like for you. If you are like me and have a fear of abandonment or rejection, begin with your earliest recollection of pain. Ask yourself what that little girl needed in the time she felt so hurt?

Write down your memory and the unmet need from the care giver in your life:

_____

_____

_____

_____

_____

Now rewrite a new memory where you experienced acceptance from that original situation:

_____

_____

Write down what you think you needed in that moment of time and possibly what the people around you needed to recognize that:

Close your eyes and imagine your adult-self giving that same acceptance to the little girl inside of you. What would you do? What would you say?

Begin to think of small ways you can advocate for yourself in your current life. Think of the different areas where your self-acceptance can grow beyond a nice idea and become an action.

List some of your commitments to nurture yourself. Look back on your previous worksheets and see some of the goals you have been working on.

How can your self-awareness help you build your self-acceptance?

_____

_____

_____

_____

_____

_____

_____

Grace is a state of being where we can extend compassion for ourselves and others even in difficult struggles. Walking in grace allows us to be connected to higher universal principles for our choices and responses to the world. One of the first lessons I learned in therapy was this nugget of truth that human beings make the best right choice for themselves in the moment of time that they make it and with the information that they have.

We as human beings are hard wired to act instinctually for survival and self-preservation. The idea that our best and even worst choices are made from a "greatest possible outcome" principle means that even in our failures we still wanted the best. Even in our parents' inadequacies and our relationship disappointments that you and the ones you love were doing the best you could with what you had.

When we extend grace towards ourselves we are reducing the shame and guilt responses and engaging freedom and respect. When we begin to allow people to be exactly as they are, make the choices that they make to live the life they want to live then we release ourselves of expectations and wasted energy. We can extend the same grace to ourselves to walk our own journey free from expectation.

In what areas of your life do you wish to extend grace to yourself and others?

_____

_____

_____

_____

_____

_____

Additional thoughts:

_____

_____

_____

_____

_____

_____

_____

Essential Oil and Grounding Intervention:

Ledum

The longer we have spent hurting or feeling stuck the deeper we can bury the simple dreams and traits of our true self. Our trusting heart that was open to the world can become closed off, distrusting, and jaded. We can experience compassion fatigue. Where we were once generous with our time, our encouragements, and our emotional investments we instead hoard feelings of resentment and fear.

The little quirky behaviors that connected us to our inner child are over shadowed with judgement and self-cynicism. At this part of your journey it is important to reconnect with the dreams and personality traits that you have set aside. To walk in gratitude, acceptance, and grace we must open our hearts. Ledum essential oil supports the body's cleaning process and emotionally helps open our hearts up to emotional availability. Moving past fear into vulnerability and courage to become reconnected to ourselves and others.

When applying Ledum we place a drop over our heart center and focus our mind towards our heart. You have been practicing listening to your heart and now you will connect that same meditation to an affirmation and new behavior. As you listen and recognize the feelings, desires, and dreams that have been wounded allow them to transform into new life, new hope, and new purpose. Our affirmation is "I open my heart to be authentic".

Now we tie the affirmation to a new behavior that supports this thought. Think of one small gesture or movement that you can do that reinforces this mental image of being open hearted. I love to pair this with the deep breathing combined with the arm movements to expand my chest and lungs. As in the first lessons I pull new life towards my heart center and breathe out the fear I carry that would rob me of joy. I rest my hands on my heart, raise them over my head and open my arms to my sides in a salutation bringing them back to rest in open palms.

I imagine my inner child dancing freely in the open spaces of the Oklahoma skies and I remind myself that I am free. I will never close my heart towards life or love again.

Write down your open-heart dream and how you will remind yourself to keep yourself free:

_____

_____

_____

_____

_____

_____

_____

_____

_____

_____

Commitments

Reflection 17: Commitment 3 -
Attunement and Mindfulness

When I was young I bought my first piano. It was a beautiful up right antique with gorgeous dark cherry wood bevels. I loved the sound of its rickety old ivory keys and though we had it tuned several times the cracks in the sound board gave it its own twang. I took lessons when I was young and though I do not practice as I should I love to sit and pluck a few keys now and again. When I was thinking of this lesson and the importance of tuning our own life this piano was the perfect picture of how trauma impacts our life.

In trauma, one of the key differences in the rehabilitation process is attunement. Attunement is the concept that you are seen and heard by someone you care about and you can see and hear that same person. In neuropsychology they talk about mirroring neuros and how the brain has a deep need to model and be modeled. This is why modeled teaching is so powerful. No matter what you say the main form of teaching is through action. Attunement is the process of knowing that someone is watching, learning, and experiencing you and that you can share that experience.

The painful part of trauma is that when the bond of attunement is not present and you do not feel seen, heard, or experienced then pain is carried in isolation. You don't feel understood. You are alone. When you do not experience attunement as a child you develop deep veins of shame and isolation that work like cracks in a sound board. No matter how many times you tune yourself to the sounds of others in your adulthood the crack comes resounding through your life. You can practice gratitude and acceptance and like me fall in love with your own unique "sounds", but the truth is that the scars of trauma are ever present. To repair my beautiful antique, we were told that we would have to replace the sound board. The same is also true in trauma. We must replace the processing of our information and scope of the world. We must rewrite our brain to experience life through attunement and mindfulness.

Mindfulness has become a popular term in therapy that really means turning your mind back to yourself in every moment that you can. Taking every action, feeling, thought and touching it with your brain. Most of the grounding lessons in this book are based on mindful practices Allowing yourself to be fully present in each moment of your life. Feeling and experiencing each moment as if it is your first time. If you made all the extra thoughts in your mind quiet and just began to think about yourself in this moment, what does it feel like to sit exactly where you are? How do the pages feel in your hands? How do your clothes feel on your body? Are you sitting or lying? Can you feel your toes? If you made your mind quiet what parts of you experience each moment of your life? Mindfulness is about knowing yourself in each breath and allowing yourself to be still and make space for you in your life. Mindfulness allows gratitude and acceptance to grow into love.

Take a few moments to turn your own attunement towards yourself. On the "Sound Board" below write down three of the cracks that you feel has changed the sound of your song. And then next to it write the way you are working to tune yourself to your true sound. Do you have any relationships that are able to hear your true sound and sing it back to you? Do you have hobbies or interests that spark joy in your heart? When do you find that you are most mindful of your presence in life? These are the moments that allow us to heal the cracks in our hearts.

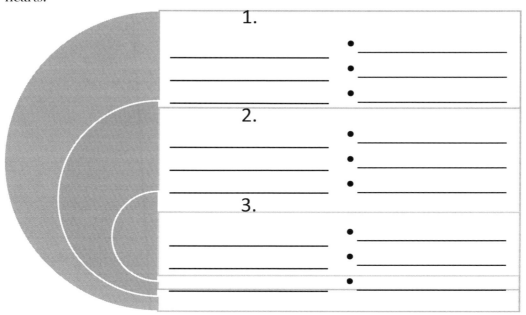

Now that you have identified some of the way you are bringing attunement into your life outline ways to infuse your life and relationships with attunement.

In what relationships would you like to increase attunement?

_____

_____

_____

In what ways will you model attunement in these relationships?

_____

_____

_____

How can you foster attunement in your home?

_____

_____

_____

How can you cultivate a work culture that supports attunement?

_____

_____

_____

What friendships allow you to experience attunement?

_____

_____

_____

The power of cultivating a life that fosters attunement is that it allows you to see and be seen in your own life, to hear and be heard. Without these basic principles our existence can become meaningless. It is exhausting to feel that we are always on the losing end of meaningless sacrifice. We are always the first one awake and the last one to bed.

I remember being a child and both my grandmother and my mother would almost never sit down and enjoy a dinner without repeated interruptions and constant trips back and forth to the kitchen to fulfill requests. It is the fine line between wanting to meet your children's needs and becoming "Cinder-mom" with no time for yourself. If you are not a mother than perhaps you can relate this to work or another relationship where you feel sloppy seconds to the needs of others.

It is easy to become numb to the disillusionment of service when we are giving and never noticed, seen, or understood for our contributions. Take the time to pour back into yourself to fill this void of attunement. Enrich your life with practices that support your autonomy and voice. Have faith that you are gifted with a unique perspective and have a purpose to share it. Allow yourself to be seen by others as authentic and sincere.

Additional thoughts:

_____

_____

_____

_____

_____

_____

_____

_____

_____

_____

Essential Oil and Grounding Intervention:

Cypress

In this section of the book our grounding interventions focus closely on the heart. Cypress oil supports the cardiovascular system in the body and engages feelings of security. The affirmation we use for Cypress is "I am free from insecurity". As we begin to turn the pages of our story and look back into how far we have come and what we have survived, feelings of inadequacy can be triggered within us. Sometimes when I think back to the experiences I have had and choices I have made there is this conflicting message of resiliency and regret.

My life's journey has been complicated and confusing, but I ground myself in the truth that we are not who we were, and we can only be who we are today. Mindfulness teaches us to be present in only the moments of now. Keeping your heart focused on this very moment allows you to remain in a position of purpose. I use Cypress topically. It is one of the oils I incorporate into massage. Take a 2-3 drops in your palm and massage them into your feet, legs, shoulders, and heart center.

Focus your mind on each muscle group and allow yourself to release the insecurities and fear that you carry. "I release my fault, my failings, and my inadequacies. I am only who I can be at the point in which I exist today. I am free to be myself." Allow yourself to stay open hearted to who you are and who you choose to be in the present moment. Allow yourself to be reinvented, repaired, reconnected, and reengaged in your life no matter what you have had to overcome to be at this moment. A flower does not regret the dark soil it had to grow through to able to bloom. Allow yourself to bloom in the space you have without apology or fear of insecurity. You are, and that is enough.

Additional thoughts:

_____

_____

_____

_____

_____

Commitments

Reflection 18: Commitment 4 -

Imagine Compassion

Our minds have a powerful way of manifesting the things we think on. This has been a huge psychological principle applied to business, sports, life, and mental health. The more you focus on something the more you are likely to see and experience it in your life. The frame of mind we operate from is how we see and experience the world. I know we have talked a lot in these lessons about having a negative mindset towards ourselves. From an early age we tend to have extreme expectations of ourselves and when we fail to live up to them we become cruel.

There is a wonderful quote by Khalil Gibran "God said "love your enemy" so I obeyed Him and loved myself". The Bible teaches that there are two great commandments. To first love God with all of your heart, soul, and mind. The second is just like the first, to love our neighbors as ourselves (Matthew 22:35-40). If you believe that God breathed His spirit into the first man created in His image. Then God's spirit was carried over into each person that lives, we each contain a fraction of God's spirit in our being. As human beings we are unique in every part of our intelligent design.

If we are created in the image of God and our great commandments are to love God and to love others. Then it is also our commandment to love ourselves which is loving God and loving others. Based on this simple command then our horrid habit of self-abuse goes against who we were created to be. We were created and commanded to love ourselves as we are created. Not to love some perfect version of ourselves or love it when we live up to some expectation. We are to simply love.

Love is difficult to know, difficult to describe, and difficult to understand. Most of what we know and understand about love is based on a human experience from individuals who don't know how to love themselves. How can we know the truth of love without a frame of reference? Someone once said to me that the bravest thing in the world is to do something in which you have no concept of. Daring to be a good parent when you haven't experienced having a good parent. Deciding to break generational cycles of abuse when everything you've ever known originated in trauma. Determining to love yourself when all you have experienced has taught you to hate yourself and others.

In the lessons leading up to this one you have been working on commitments that would create a foundation to becoming open to self-love. We started with small steps of gratitude and acceptance. Learning to tune our hearts to listen to our own song. Now we begin to meditate and imagine compassion.

With an open heart I want you to begin turning your mind to compassion. How would you define compassion?

_____

_____

_____

Have you ever experienced compassion?

_____

_____

_____

Is there anyone that you naturally feel compassion for or towards?

_____

_____

_____

Spend time meditating on compassion as a visual representation. Think of compassion as a color, a visual concept of compassion. Think of compassion as a person, a reference for what visible evidence of compassion you have seen. Think of compassion as a sensation, an emotional response of belonging and hope.

Where would you feel this sensation in your body?

How would it feel in your mind?

Would you have any thoughts about this experience?

Write down what thoughts come to your mind about compassion.

_____

_____

_____

_____

_____

_____

_____

_____

Finally, how does compassion for yourself affect your faith? How does your higher power demonstrate compassion for you?

_____

_____

_____

_____

_____

_____

_____

The next part is engaging that principle of psychology we talked about at the start of the lesson. Using our mind to manifest experiences in our lives. Commit to spending time every day imagining compassion for these 5 groups of people in your life. How will you bring love into your thoughts towards yourself and others? In your mind, paint a picture of compassion and write or draw what you see. The compassion you share with yourself and your relationships returns to you.

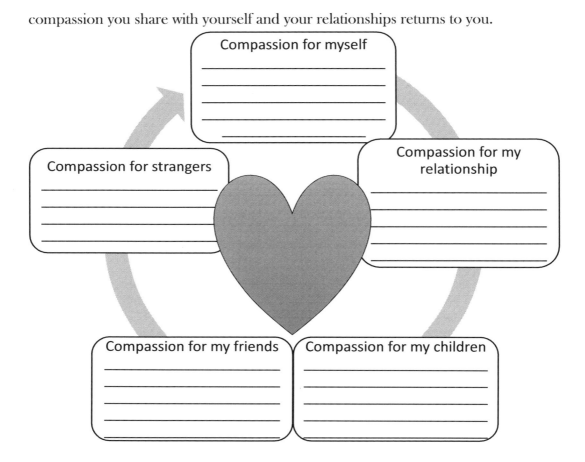

Essential Oil and Grounding Intervention:

Lavender

These delicate moments of beginning to love ourselves may create feelings of uncertainty and even confusion. For me I would hold back happiness afraid that if I experienced too much joy somehow the "other shoe would drop" or I would wake up to find it wasn't real. I guarded my heart from experiencing the joy of being authentic and free. I would take steps towards love but hold on to my anxiety waiting for the moment that my fear would say "I told you so, you don't deserve love or happiness". If you find yourself wrestling this these thoughts know that you are exactly where you should be in your journey. You are growing and changing your patterns and that can feel terrifying for your brain.

Reach for your essential oils, I like to use Lavender as it has powerful neurological support properties to reduce feelings of anxiety and fear of abandonment. Our affirmation is "I am loved, and I belong". Place a drop of lavender in your hand to breathe deeply and as you state your affirmation. "I am loved and belong to myself, I am loved and belong to the world, I am loved and belong to life". Because I struggled with abandonment and rejection this is an affirmation I still use today. I remind myself that my purpose and potential create space for my gifts in the world. To exist without anxiety and to release control of the measure of compassion. To not limit the joy and happiness I allow my heart to receive, to be open to see and be seen.

Take time to meditate on compassion towards the 5 groups in this lesson. Begin with the sensation of compassion inside of you and how you would experience that in your heart. Allow that sensation to grow and keep that alive in you. As we begin to open our hearts and invite compassion into our imaginations, creativity comes alive in us once again and we see ourselves as we were designed.

Additional thoughts:

_____

_____

_____

_____

_____

_____

_____

_____

_____

_____

Commitments

Reflection 19: Commitment 5 -
Meeting Our Basic Needs

Beautiful friend, stop and take a moment to recognize how very courageous you are to continue to work on yourself, to make commitments for change in your life. To spend the last few weeks building yourself up as a person, to live in authenticity and grace. Many women will wish for a better life and make changes for their children or spouses but minimize the work they could do to fill their own hearts with joy. This work we have done together has been a shift in mindset, lifestyle, and perspective and positioned you to continue to grow yourself in search of your dreams.

Most people build their lives on broken dreams and never realize that by burying their pain they lose themselves. Sometimes we live in the illusions of helplessness, "stuckness", or hopelessness. We say things that belittle our own power for change, "I am not good enough", "this is all I deserve", or allow our regrets to dictate our futures. It is easy to cast off our responsibility for self-work on failures or faulty beliefs. But we are the active agents in our life and our commitments are the guiding force in who we become. I am so proud of you, keep moving forward and continue to evolve.

In the very first lesson we outlined the concept on unmet needs feeding fears in our lives. You spent some time writing down some of the needs you have in your life. Again, in lesson 13 we listed the strengths we have in meeting our own needs. Now, in this lesson we will learn how keeping a strong foundation of needs met in our lives allows us to reach our true authentic self. The fundamental power of who we are comes from building blocks of self-care. In Maslow's hierarchy of needs the outline of the five basic human needs of all individuals, survival, safety, love/belonging, meaning/purpose, and self-actualization. To discover your true self, you must have each of these fundamental building blocks in your life. These are the basic needs of every individual regardless of culture, background, experience, or faith. These needs, if unmet or broken can create suffering within the psychological processing on the person. One of the reasons trauma is so dangerous to the psychological process is that it breaks our sense of safety and survival. Even substance abuse and other mental health disorders can bring an individual to experience life from a survival instinct with all their basic needs compromised.

In the healing process we are challenged to build our life back up on these foundational supports. In each of the lessons we have worked through so far, they can be tied to creating a life of safety, belonging, and love. Once we can find and build compassion in our life our next step is to find meaning and purpose in who we are and what we have experienced. Meaningfulness is the purpose in which we assign to our behaviors and actions. To be authentic you must take responsibility for your happiness and your suffering. The moment that I recognized the purpose I had in my life

and the meaningfulness behind all my choices I was able to find value in both the positive and the regret ridden decisions I had made. I could choose to learn from each experience and let the pain leave the memory.

I think it is important to note the importance of accepting responsibility for our responses to our trauma and pain. If we were honest with ourselves, then we would see things we could have done to have altered our journey. We are responsible to build emotional resiliency and support mental health hygiene to life full hearted and well. We are not able to avoid trauma in our lives, but we can learn from our experiences and allow them to build compassion, empathy, and purpose.

Maybe like me, you would find that your childhood trauma created cycles of relationships that kept you lost and in pain, but the truth is I knew that I kept myself in pain longer than I needed to be. I used my sadness to hurt myself and played small apologizing for my existence. Living in a way that honors our authentic self, we can determine how we cope, how we recover, and how our recovery is meaningful.

What would your old self say to the new person you are today?

_____

_____

_____

_____

_____

_____

_____

_____

_____

_____

When you think of your future self what do you hope for in her life 5 years from now?

_____

_____

_____

_____

_____

_____

_____

_____

_____

What meaningful experiences have you discovered through this journey of change?

_____

_____

_____

_____

_____

_____

_____

_____

_____

_____

_____

_____

What new purpose do you feel is driving you?

_____

_____

_____

_____

_____

_____

_____

_____

_____

_____

_____

_____

_____

_____

_____

_____

_____

_____

_____

_____

_____

_____

_____

What commitments have you made to fulfill your purpose as an authentic woman?

_____

_____

_____

_____

_____

_____

_____

_____

_____

_____

_____
_____
_____
_____
_____
_____
_____

Additional Thoughts:

_____
_____
_____
_____
_____
_____
_____
_____
_____
_____
_____

Essential Oil and Grounding Intervention:

Ylang Ylang

You could spend a lifetime learning about the divine spark inside of yourself and it would not be a life wasted. We women possess so many amazing attributes and qualities and as you walk in your purpose you can experience stretching of your abilities and gifts. It can be emotionally exhausting to grow internally especially when those around us are not aware of this internal process. For this intervention reach for the bottle of the beautiful exotic Ylang Ylang. Stress and exhaustion are a natural part of growth and accomplishment. When we reach this place learn to rest.

Take a drop of Ylang Ylang essential oil on your palm, breathe it in and find a comfortable place to lay flat on your back, elevate your feet above your heart and allow yourself to be still. As you close your eyes imagine your body becoming heavy, as you breathe out each breath allow your stomach to lower and feel the weight of your stress sink through you and down through the floor below you. Breathe in rest and let go of scarcity. Our affirmation is "I have what I need".

Plan your day to include brief rest periods of 10-minute increments to elevate your legs and increase your breathing specifically in times when you are experiencing stress. Allow yourself to have what you need to be your best self through this process of growth.

Additional thoughts:

_____

_____

_____

_____

_____

_____

_____

_____

Commitments

Reflection 20: Commitment 6 -

Fundamentals of Happiness

Happiness has been a lost art for me most of my adult life. What does happiness even mean? It is a sensation, an accomplishment, or mindset? I had believed that happiness was unattainable and a terrible goal to build your life around. Every new life task seemed laden with struggle and stress, I couldn't imagine happiness being an active part of my life. My closest ideas around what attaining happiness would look like were an eternal vacation spot in my mind. Arriving at a destination that would no longer include struggle or suffering.

My goal to reach happiness was to end the suffering in my life and that just seemed impossible. So, "let's just give up on ideas of happiness". I didn't realize that was my trauma speaking broken truth in my life. Then, one day I heard happiness explained differently I still believe happiness is an unattainable destination, because it isn't a destination at all. It is a way of being. A lifestyle, I will explain.

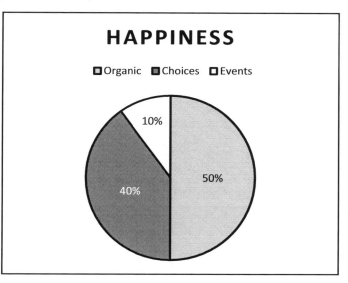

Life is difficult and filled with adversity. Every part of life that is new or challenging includes stress, discomfort, and fear. I am sure that even in your life, during the time you have been working through this book that you have experienced some difficult challenge or are suffering through some trouble. Every person that is living struggles in life to one degree or another. The goal is not to cease suffering, the goal is how you are responding to life and all its struggles. Are you taking responsibility for your suffering, for your happiness, for your emotions?

In a class I heard happiness laid out in a diagram that helped me create a clear idea of this concept. The instructor said that 50% of happiness came from an internal place. It was organic, biological, or genetic. This is coming from your body or brain. This can be supported by supporting your brain and body to stay healthy. Eating, drinking, sleeping, and living well. This is the part that medications and exercise can make an impact on. Then 40% of our happiness comes from our choices. Our character, lifestyle, and habits. This we can increase or decrease with simple small changes to our life. Then he said that 10% of our happiness is from events and relationships outside of us. Only 10% of our happiness or unhappiness do we actually have no control over. This was very powerful to hear. This meant that the choice I was making to avoid happiness was based on only 10% of my potential experience of happiness. I had missed the 90% of my responsibility to cultivate myself and my emotions. I was 90% responsible for my own happiness and I had dropped the ball and blamed others for my deficits. Talk about a gut punch.

About two year ago I acquired a small chicken coop with a flock of 9 birds. I had never owned chickens and for the most part was intimidated by them. I was very excited about the possibilities of keeping breakfast producing animals and I had heard of the benefits for gardening that chickens provide. What I completely under estimated was how much happiness chickens would bring to my life and how much they would teach me about God. Over the last two years I have fallen in love with these clucky feathery animals. I don't pretend to understand why I love these simple creatures so much.

When I tell people that I have chickens they look at me as if I might be crazy and I agree with them. All that chickens do is peck the ground and poop out eggs. They are such simple creatures but each one is unique and has its own personality. I have started naming them based on their disposition; I have a Lady Bird, Glinda, Bonnie, Izzy, Frenchie, Betty, Dorothy, Marshmallow, General Patton, and Mr. Whiskers. They are always getting out of their pen, crowing all around our house, digging up my newly planted roses but, when I sit outside I find such peace and happiness just being in the garden with them and after a long day I can't wait to be out there with them. I believe this is how God feels about us, he can't wait to walk with us, to laugh at our silliness, and shake his head at our shenanigans. If I can love chickens this much and they can fill my heart with so much laughter, I only imagine how much God loves us. He can't wait to just sit and be with us and enjoy our individuality as He created us, our authentic self.

Begin thinking of your Happiness Chart, think about the ways you can build the organic happiness in your life. What is your body facing to provide you a balanced positive mindset that can produce responses based in joy? Are you supportive of your organic body through your diet, exercise, and sleep? Do you have any genetic challenges or mental health struggles? Are there responsibilities you can take to provide your body what it needs to help you experience more happiness in your life? This is half of your happiness experiences that you can begin to affect through small steps to build your body's responses. Note simple steps to build your body up in the chart below. Maybe that is a simple step of taking your medication, or using your oils, or getting the 8 hours of sleep you need every day.

Now we will focus on the choices that we can make to build our happiness. Are you taking responsibilities for your choices to be happy? We can wake up and read post-it notes of affirmations on our bathroom mirrors and those are helpful but thinking about choosing happiness is only the first step. We must act. We must do small things that really bring happiness alive in our lives. For me that was chickens, gardening, and sharing oils with those I love. I believe there is a strong connection to growing things and a sense of fulfillment, belonging, and purpose. Write down some things that build the sensation of happiness for you. Be mindful of what is realistic. I am sure goats and other farm animals would also bring me happiness, but it would not bring my husband any joy. In fact, I think he would resent me building a petting zoo in our backyard, so I set realistic goals for my happiness. Be mindful of the life you are building and the relationships you value. What can you choose to cultivate happiness?

Lastly, take note of the individuals, events, and situations outside of your control that bring you happiness. It may be easier to think of the events that have brought unhappiness and use that to outline what would be a better experience. I am sure we would all put down events surrounding vacations and life changing moments but try to think of things that might happen more regularly. Things that you can build into your life daily. What events, moments, or relationships can you look to for happiness in every day?

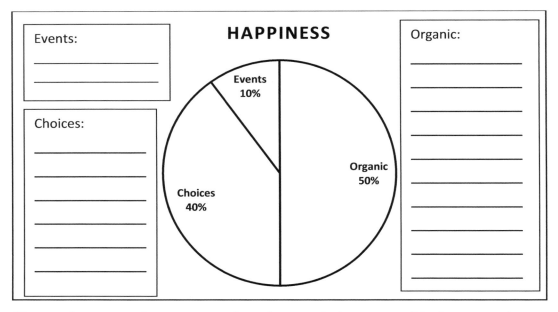

Now, make a commitment to your happiness, to being responsible for supporting your life in a direction that allows your happiness to flourish internally. So much of happiness begins with showing up for your own life, taking risks, doing small things you enjoy daily, and staying connected to your inner self. Take time to cultivate new experiences, go out and buy chickens, grow things, and allow 90% of you to be responsible for where you are and the choices you make.

"I will commit to my individual happiness by honoring my organic self and my authentic self. I will open my heart up to happiness by remaining connected to me. I will bring my greatest gifts and blessings forward every morning as I walk in my unique purpose for my life. I will over flow with joy and spill out onto others."

Additional thoughts:

_____

_____

_____

_____

_____

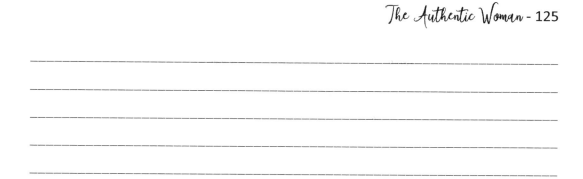

Essential Oil and Grounding Intervention:

Lime

Can you begin to imagine the amount of joy and happiness you bring to this world, this garden, to our creator? Does it make you smile to know that you are seen and understood, valued and treasured? The commitment to happiness was a huge step for me in my journey and even today one that I feel I have not mastered. Life has a way of causing us to lose sight of ourselves. Lime essential oil is an amazingly fresh and cheerful scent that can re-center our focus back to ourselves.

Our affirmation is "I see myself". Take a few moments to meditate on being seen. This can be a triggering thought but important to focus on as we begin to grow. Allow yourself and your higher power the pleasure of seeing yourself. For this intervention look into a mirror, at your face, at your body and speak your affirmation. "I see you, I see myself. I am seen by my higher power to walk in my design". Spend at least 5 minutes looking at yourself deeply. What truth do you see?

Life might not always be happy, and this mediation may not be easy but as we discussed in the previous lessons basing our identity and thoughts on truth is critical for our healing. See yourself in truth and allow that truth to be a foundation for your choices.

Happiness has become tied to truth statements in my life. I deserve happiness, I choose happiness, I bring happiness. These are some of my truth statements that allow me to value myself even in hardship or struggle. Write your truth statements and allow yourself to meditate on what you see in yourself.

Truth statement 1:

_____

_____

_____

Truth statement 2:

_____

_____

_____

Truth statement 3:

_____

_____

_____

Additional thoughts:

_____

_____

_____

_____

_____

_____

_____

_____

_____

Commitments

Reflection 21: Commitment 7 -

The Authentic You

Lesson 21, your journey is just beginning. It is my hope that you have been incorporating each of these lessons into your life and now feeling a bit more empowered. Walking every day with purpose and falling in love with the person you are and are becoming. Take just a moment to speak a truth about yourself that you have learned. Recognize this truth and hold it close. You are the catalyst for change; you are the reason for hope; you are the gift.

In this last lesson I want to talk to you about failure and success. You are on your journey and how you meet success and failure is incredibly important, any person that sets out to live life fully will experience both. It is critical to note that these two concepts are not opposite forces. I want to challenge you to be careful not to spend too much thought on polarizing yourself into a "one or the other" kind of experience.

The opposite of failure is not success, the opposite of failure is growth. Any moment of our life that can allow us to learn, change, or reconnect is an opportunity for growing. In fact, the idea of failure is almost irrelevant if we remain open hearted and humble as women. Every lesson in this book has been designed to shift your mindset back towards living a life of passion and purpose. It is not to promise a worry free or forever rose-colored glasses existence but the promise of personal freedom through authentic interactions. Opening to a mindset of growth negates the idea of failure.

I write this last chapter and see how even in the process of creating these worksheets has challenged me to expand a growth mindset towards myself. If you are like me it can be easy to be encouraging and supportive of our families, friends, and even strangers. I find that it is hardest to extend grace to myself especially if I am caught in a success verses failure conflict.

So how do we grow in grace? As I conclude this journey of writing this book, I think of how you will be holding my heart between these pages. The message I have for you is grace. To be authentic to me means that we allow ourselves to grow in grace every day, not perfection and free from judgement. You have everything inside of yourself that you need to grow into exactly who you are meant to be. If you are free from judgement then you are free from the outcome of success or failure, you need only to exist. Think of yourself as a force of nature, a strong force. As we said at the beginning of this book Murphy's Law "An object in motion will remain in motion unless met by an equal or opposite force". You are the force of life. You will remain in motion and become a greater force than anything that has come against you. Success is not the force that stops us, and neither is failure. If you measure your life in achievements then you are only as big or small as what you do, the goals you set, and the tasks you complete.

Being goal oriented is a positive behavior that allows us to move our life in a direction of our choosing, but it should never define our existence. We all want to experience success but again releasing ourselves from this outcome allows us to walk in authenticity and grace. Take a moment to think and write what it means to you to be your "authentic self":

_____

_____

_____

_____

_____

_____

_____

Now, take this defined, heart centered purpose and frame it into your life, your obligations, and your goal-oriented world. How do you grow in grace as your true self while living out your commitments? In this final worksheet we will create a mind map. This might not be a large enough scale and you may need to create a version online or even by hand. I found a software called XMind to do mine, but I think you could draw or create your own rather easily.

In the chart below write down your "Authentic Self" definition for your life. What it means to be you, to have your heart, and what message your heart carries for the world. Now section off each category of your life and i.e. family, career, self. Other good categories might include Recovery, Spirituality, Education, any life pursuit.

Under each of those main focuses create goals that honor your life purpose. Break down each subtopic to include the tasks you do that carry out these obligations in a growth mindset. How do you embody your authentic self in your daily life? Finally, write your desires for each task, goal, and category. Be careful to notice and remove expectations of outcomes or measures of success because they give finality to our growth potential.

They limit us from all that we could become. Remember that life happens spherically and all at once, every day you are baring all these desires and stresses to embody the person you are. You have purpose and passion; judgement of success or failure has no part of your future.

Building a growth mindset means that you are always finding new ways to support yourself and learn from every experience. I would take this one step further and say that when you have an authentic mindset you cultivate internal growth and allow who you are to become manifested in every part of your life. You leave an imprint of your soul on the relationships you invest in and the connections you create.

As you add to your mind map and develop each frame work for your life you can assess how your time is being invested in the desires of your heart and the opportunities you must live out your true self. Even small tasks such as household chores and paying bills can become an expression of your whole hearted existence. You are no longer a lost and hurting person simply reacting to the pain you feel, you are the active agent of a true authentic life. Live it in grace.

Additional thoughts:

_____

_____

_____

_____

_____

_____

_____

_____

_____

_____

_____

_____

_____

Essential Oil and Grounding Intervention:

Palo Santo

Emotional balance through daily support is an act of love that empowers us to be our best self. Every lesson you have applied from this book is one that you can continue and expand upon daily. When I was a child my parents taught me the word sincerity. When potters throw clay on a wheel to make a vessel it is an incredibly tedious and difficult task. The clay is molded and shaped slowly and with great care. Every time the potter's hand snags on a lump of clay the potter must stop the wheel and remove it. That small clump once removed leaves a crevasse or weak spot in the clay. The potter will tear down the vessel and begin to reshape it.

A potter could repeat the process several times per vessel. Some potters do not take the trouble to do this. They simply remove the lump in the clay and fill the hole with wax. The unsuspecting buyer would not be able to tell if a bowl or vase had wax on it once painted. A potter could skip all the work it would take to tear down and build up their pieces and even lower their prices since they were able to shorten their time working on the wheel. Taking short cuts compromised the quality of their vessels and when used in the ovens to cook with these vessels cracked under the heat because of the wax filled holes.

True potters who took the time to work their clay to a state of perfection began to mark their work "Sincere" which means without wax. As you are building up your life meditate of all the times you feel that you are tearing down your life and building yourself up again to be sincere. For this we use a drop of Palo Santo, "Holy Stick", a beautiful aroma when diffused or applied topically that can help ignite your spirit and light a fire within your heart. As you are the vessel carrying the oil of life to bring light to the world, keep that fire burning and allow it to be a passion that drives you forward. As you breathe remember all that you are and everything you are becoming.

Additional thoughts:

_____

_____

_____

_____

Your Authentic Self Narrative

I want you to not conclude your journey in healing as you conclude this book but use it as a building block on your journey. I want you to remember that your mindset about your healing process is just as important as the actions and activities you do surrounding your healing. Building daily practices that allows you to keep your heart open to development and healing throughout your life and extend that healing to others.

Wellness is a lifestyle and wholeness is not an accomplishment but rather a continual process of regulation and support. You are not arriving at a life well-ordered free from chaos, but rather a vessel moving back and forth with the tides of life between peace and suffering, order and chaos. Think back to each of the sections you have completed, all that you have learned about yourself, all that you have overcome to be the amazing person you are.

You are a force of strength, power, and peace. You are learning every day to walk in forgiveness and extend grace to yourself first and then others. You are committed to gratitude and acceptance so that love can flourish in your life. You are practicing your grounding tools and using oils to focus on how just as tiny drops of faith we overflow our hearts to pour out to others. I am so honored to have been a small part of your journey.

It is my prayer that you take these lessons and continue to grow, share, and build on them. This last portion I dedicate to the transformed self.

In this last narrative write about you, The Authentic Woman.

_____

_____

_____

_____

_____

_____

_____

_____

Where to Go from Here

Share:

As you close the last chapter of this book it is my challenge to you that your story not remain on these pages but that you take what you have learned from this book and begin to share it. As you walk in your freedom you begin to allow other women to experience the grace and gratitude that you are practicing. You were created for an amazing purpose and the world is waiting for you to take your place in its story.

Every day that you walk in authenticity even in the smallest acts of genuine kindness, remain open hearted and allow others to experience you. Use your oils every day and I would encourage you to share what you have learned about oils as well.

Somewhere in my journey I began not just dropping them on my skin but also sharing them with friends so that they could experience them. I have enclosed a short message for individuals that would like to use this workbook in a group setting to share with teams, book studies, or therapy groups.

Lead:

If you are using this as a guided group study I would encourage participants to work individually on lessons and practice the mediations in a group setting while sharing the personal insight they gained from the worksheets. In my group practice I use Young Living Essential Oils to facilitate the deep breathing meditations and we as a group engage in the cupping exercises. I have a brief section addressing essential oils in the opening of the book with addition research available for further reading.

If you would like to know about how I use oils in my private practice, please reach out to me. The power of meditation with aroma therapy helps create the therapeutic environment before and after deep emotional processing. I love being able to incorporate this into my practice to provide a unique experience for clients. I pray you also remember to keep these oils close and apply them to yourself as you continue your great work.

Oil Up:

Remember that it matters what you put in your body, in your mind, and in your life. You alone can make the changes that remove toxic relationships, toxic behaviors, and even toxic products. Make a change for your life and live differently. Join our Young Living tribe and learn more about experiencing freedom through aromatherapy. Order your started kit today at www.youngliving.com add in my member number 2740692 for sponsor and enroller. We would be honored to help guide your journey and help you stay learn and grow.

Connect:

Join our community on social media platforms: Facebook Tara Nichols & Instagram @taraenichols

Connect through our website: www.taranichols.com

Email me at: mentalhealth.taranichols@gmail.com

Join our oils team: www.myyl.com/holistichope

Sources and Additional Reading

Articles and Studies:

Al-Harrasi A., Csuk R., Khan A., Hussain J. *Distribution of the anti-inflammatory and anti-depressant compounds: Incensole and incensole acetate in genus Boswellia.* 2019 May; 161:28-40. doi: 10.1016/j.phytochem.2019.01.007. Epub 2019 Feb 22. Retrieved from: https://www.ncbi.nlm.nih.gov/pubmed/30802641

Wang S, Wang C, Yu Z, Wu C, Peng D, Liu X, Liu Y, Yang Y, Guo P, Wei J. *Agarwood Essential Oil Ameliorates Restrain Stress-Induced Anxiety and Depression by Inhibiting HPA Axis Hyperactivity.* 2018 Nov 5;19(11). pii: E3468. doi: 10.3390/ijms19113468. Retrieved from: https://www.ncbi.nlm.nih.gov/pubmed/30400578

Kumar Y, Prakash O, Tripathi H, Tandon S, Gupta MM, Rahman LU, Lal RK, Semwal M, Darokar MP, Khan F. AromaDb: *A Database of Medicinal and Aromatic Plant's Aroma Molecules With Phytochemistry and Therapeutic Potentials.* Front Plant Sci. 2018 Aug 13;9:1081. doi: 10.3389/fpls.2018.01081. eCollection 2018. Retrieved from: https://www.ncbi.nlm.nih.gov/pubmed/30150996

Books on Essential Oils:

Chemistry of Essential Oils Made Simple: God's Love Manifest in Molecules Hardcover (2005) by David Stewart

Healing Oils of the Bible (2003) by David Stewart

Essential Oils Desk Reference, Seventh Edition (2016) Life Science Products and Publishing

The Miracle of Essential Oils: Harnessing the Power of Botanicals to Ease Physical, Emotional and Psychological Trauma (2017) by Watson M.Ed., Ryan, Jason Sapp, et al.

Releasing Emotional Patterns with Essential Oils: Thirteenth Edition 2019. Carolyn L. Mein

Additional Therapeutic Resources:

Buddha's Brain: The Practical Neuroscience of Happiness, Love, and Wisdom. November 1, 2009 by Rick Hanson, Richard Mendius

The Body Keeps the Score: Brain, Mind, and Body in the Healing of Trauma. Sep, 2014 by Bessel Van der Kolk MD, Sean Pratt, et al.

Fortitude – Rising Out of the Trenches of Trauma into a Life Free from Fear, Pain, Shame and Suicidal Thoughts. June 2019 by Jason Sapp, MATS with Stephani La'Nette Sapp

12 Rules for Life: An Antidote to Chaos by Jordan B. Peterson (Author, Narrator), Norman Doidge MD - foreword (Author), Random House Canada (Publisher)

Reconciliation: Healing the Inner Child Paperback – Thich Nhat Hanh (Author) October 9, 2006

About the Author:

Tara Nichols holds a Masters in Mental Health Counseling, is a Licensed Associate Professional Counselor at The Psychology Center, and raises her family in Douglasville, Georgia. Mrs. Nichols is dedicated to living in wellness focusing on the whole individual as an active agent in their own journey. Mrs. Nichols works specifically with women and children's issues and focuses on overcoming trauma, anxiety, depression, addiction, and other disorders to live life in wellness. Using cognitive and experiential therapy interventions paired with the power of essential oils allows for therapeutic healing and building daily practices of wellness and supports the individual to live in freedom over pain, loss, and suffering. Mrs. Nichols uses aromatherapy daily to support her own wellness journey and incorporates essential oils in her therapeutic work to support healing for clients. Mrs. Nichols founded the Nichols Center, Inc and continues to aid her community in advocacy for mental health and addiction recovery. You will find Mrs. Nichols spends most of her free time with her family or in her garden with her chickens.

"My garden has given me a deeper understanding of meaningfulness and intentionality. Learning to notice myself and cultivating love and happiness just as I would for my plants, animals, and children. To be authentic we must embrace who we are and move our lives forward in commitments to our heart centered focus. If we are buried in pain, loss, and regret we cannot engage our lives in meaningfulness and purpose. This self-help workbook is a journey through my own self-reflections of trauma and healing. In these pages it is my hope to share with you how I have learned to walk open-hearted towards the life I am creating in my path towards becoming an authentic woman." -Tara Nichols

Contact Me:

Join our community on social media platforms: Facebook Tara Nichols & Instagram @taraenichols

Connect through our website: www.taranichols.com

Email me at: mentalhealth.taranichols@gmail.com

Join our essential oils team: www.myyl.com/holistichope